GCSE (9-1)

Edexcel Religio

3RB0 (Short Course)

Area of Study 1

From a Christian Perspective

Area of Study 2

From an Islamic Perspective

Brian Poxon

Edexcel Religious Studies B (Short Course)

Area of Study 1: from a Christian Perspective

Area of Study 2: from an Islamic Perspective

© 2018 Brian Poxon. All rights reserved.

This book is protected under the copyright laws of the United Kingdom. Any reproduction or other unauthorised use of the material or artwork herein is prohibited without the express written permission of the author.

While the author has used his best efforts in preparing this book, he makes no representations or warranties with respect to the accuracy or completeness of the contents of this book and specifically disclaims any implied warranties of merchantability or fitness for a particular purpose.

Neither Author nor Publisher shall be held liable for any loss or damages, including, but not limited to, special, incidental, consequential or other damages. The reader takes full responsibility for the physiological, psychological, emotional, career and financial decisions that they may or may not make after reading as well as any consequences.

References are included from the Oxford English Dictionary, some meanings are omitted, changed slightly or added to. Bible quotes refer to the New International Version.

978-1-78484-210-9 (pbk)

978-1-78484-211-6 (hbk)

978-1-78484-212-3 (ebk)

978-1-78484-213-0 (Kindle)

Published in the United Kingdom by PushMe Press

www.pushmepress.com

How to Use this Book

Students studying the Edexcel GCSE Religious Studies (short Course) choose two religions to study. This revision guide focuses on **CHRISTIANITY** for Area of Study 1 and **ISLAM** for Area of Study 2.

Each Area of Study has a 50 minute examination, meaning students take two examinations at the end of the course, both worth 50% of the qualification.

This book provides you with detailed summaries of all parts of the Pearson Edexcel B (Short Course) specification from both Christian and Islamic perspectives. It is organised according to the specification so that you can find topics easily.

At the beginning of each chapter, you will find a list of key words and their definitions. Many of these key words are in BOLD in the text so that you can see them used in context. In places, other words are highlighted as prompts for you to remember the content.

You will find advice on preparing for the exam and how to answer the questions on our website.

Area of Study 1
Religion & Ethics

(3RB0/1A-1G)

Christian Beliefs

Marriage & the Family

From a Christian perspective

Christian Beliefs

Area of Study 1 - Christian Beliefs

KEYWORDS

- **ASCENSION** - Jesus being taken up to heaven forty days after his resurrection

- **ATONEMENT** - Being made right with God

- **AUTHORITY** - Having power to give guidance, commands and direction

- **BIBLE** - Christian holy book or Scriptures, made up of the Old and New Testaments

- **CREATION** - The process of how something came into existence

- **ESCHATOLOGY** - The study of the end of the world or "end times"

- **ETERNAL** - Lasting forever; having no beginning or end; outside of time

- **EVIL** - Wicked, morally wrong, bad: natural evil caused by nature; moral evil caused by humanity

- **FORGIVENESS** - To grant pardon for an offence or sin

- **HEAVEN** - Spiritual realm thought to be the abode of God; the good afterlife

- **HELL** - Spiritual realm of punishment or the absence of God; the bad afterlife

- **IMMORTAL** - Living forever, never dying or decaying

- **INCARNATION** - Taking human form; God taking human form in Jesus

- **NICENE CREED** - An important statement of Christian belief originating in AD325 and still stated in Christian churches today

- **OMNIBENEVOLENT** - All loving

- **OMNIPOTENT** - All powerful

- **OMNIPRESENT** - Present everywhere
- **OMNISCIENT** - All knowing
- **ORIGINAL SIN** - The belief that humans are born with sin because of Adam and Eve's original disobedience to God
- **PASSION** - The last days of Jesus' life, including his suffering
- **RESURRECTION** - Jesus rising from the dead; overcoming death
- **SACRAMENT** - An event or ceremony where God's grace is received
- **SALVATION** - Deliverance from sin
- **SIN** - Anything that goes against God's law
- **SOUL** - The spiritual, non-physical and immortal part of a human
- **STEWARDSHIP** - To look after something that has been entrusted to your care
- **SUFFERING** - Undergoing pain, distress or hardship
- **TRINITY** - God the Father, Son and Holy Spirit

THE TRINITY

It is important to stress that Christians do not believe in three Gods, but one God shown in three equal ways, or three Persons. The Nicene Creed states that Christians **BELIEVE IN ONE GOD**, known as God the Father, God the Son and God the Holy Spirit. This is known as The Trinity.

- **THE FATHER** - In the Nicene Creed, God the Father is described as Almighty, and the Maker of everything, including the universe, heaven and earth. Roman Catholics believe that the Father is outside of time - eternal. Protestants believe God is everlasting inside of time. The word Father combines both the idea of authority and care, which is important for Christians when they worship God because they believe God is Almighty and All Loving at the same time

- **THE SON** - In the Nicene Creed Jesus is described as the "only-begotten Son of God, eternally begotten" (eternally begotten mean Jesus has, like God, always existed and is unique, rather than the idea of God giving birth to Jesus). Jesus is both Divine (God) and human. He lived on earth and showed people how God wants them to live, suffered and died to forgive sins and was resurrected to show that God has the power to rise from the dead. Christians believe Jesus will judge all people on Judgement Day. In worship, Christians will often joyfully express their thanks to Jesus for being willing to suffer and give his life for them to "save them", and enable them to be forgiven

- **THE HOLY SPIRIT** - After Jesus rose from the dead, he said that the Holy Spirit would come to give people guidance, and live with and in them as God's continuing presence on earth. The Nicene Creed describes the Holy Spirit as the "Lord and Giver of Life". The Holy Spirit gives comfort, peace and help, and inspires and guides Christians as they try to put beliefs into action. Christians believe that the Holy Spirit is omnipresent and by the Holy Spirit, God is with people today, enabling them to have a relationship with Him

The Trinity is very important in Christian worship. Christians believe that the Holy Spirit helps them to have a relationship with God the Father as the Holy Spirit is God's presence on earth. That relationship with the Father is possible because God the Son has died to forgive sins and therefore broken down the barrier between God and humanity.

In **CHARISMATIC CHURCHES**, emphasis in worship is for a personal experience of God, and it is believed that a person can be "filled with the Holy Spirit". Charismatic services often stress that people can receive the "gifts of the Holy Spirit" such as healing and a language known as "tongues" to help communicate more closely with God.

Even though the word **TRINITY** is not mentioned in the Bible, The Trinity working as Three Persons in Unity can be seen in New Testament passages such as Matthew, Chapter 3 verses 13-17. As Jesus is baptised, the Holy Spirit comes to Him, and, at the same time, the Father speaks. Later in Matthew's Gospel, Jesus told his disciples to baptise people in the name of **THE FATHER**, **THE SON** and **THE HOLY SPIRIT**.

THE CREATION AND HUMANITY

Christians believe that God created the entire universe. The creation of the earth and humanity is outlined in **GENESIS** Chapters 1-3. The word Genesis means **BEGINNINGS**, and many Christians believe God created the universe "out of nothing" (**EX NIHILO**).

Genesis Chapter 1, one of two creation accounts, says that the creation took place over 6 days, starting with heavens, earth, light and darkness (day 1), sky and water (day 2), land, seas and vegetation (day 3), sun, moon and stars (day 4), fish and birds (day 5), land animals and humans (day 6). Uniquely, humans are created **IN THE IMAGE OF GOD**, which makes them capable of having a relationship with God, and they are given responsibility to "rule over" the earth.

- **CREATIONISM** - Some Christians take this story literally, and believe God created the world in six 24-hour days. This belief is called Creationism. Creationists do not accept the scientific view of the universe developing over billions of years after the Big Bang

- **BIG BANG** - Other Christians believe that the creation story is not supposed to be factually accurate, but interpreted metaphorically. They would accept that God created the earth, but that could have been through the Big Bang, with evolution being the process through which life on earth developed

Christians believe that the Trinity existed before the universe and was involved in its creation. God the Father commands the universe to exist through his word. John Chapter 1 verse 1 describes Jesus as God's Word, and in John 1:3 that God the Father created all things through God the Son, his word. In Genesis 1, The Holy Spirit is also described as present and "hovering over the waters", and many Christians see the Holy Spirit as the breath of God which gives life to everything.

Genesis 3 describes how after the earth and humans were formed, God and Adam and Eve had a perfect relationship until Adam and Eve chose to disobey God. This introduced sin into the world, and is known as The Fall.

The Creation story is very important to Christians today because:

- **OMNIPOTENT** - It says that God is Omnipotent and that the world was planned by and is important to God

- **PURPOSE** - The world has a purpose and that nature and all life should be respected and cared for

- **UNIQUE** - Humans are unlike any other creatures as the creation story says that only humans were "breathed into" by God, giving them a soul. This means they have a vital role to fulfil their responsibilities which comes from them being made in the image of God. This care for the world on God's behalf is known as stewardship

- **RELATIONSHIP** - Christians believe that, uniquely, humanity can have a relationship with God

THE INCARNATION

The word incarnation refers to a person who embodies a God or Deity. Christians believe that Jesus is God in human form. He is both fully God and fully human at the same time. The Old Testament says that a Messiah or deliverer would come to save or "rescue" humanity. Jesus is the Messiah who was incarnated - literally **TOOK ON FLESH** - to live on earth, teaching and showing people how God wants them to live.

Jesus was born to Mary after she was made pregnant through the Holy Spirt, and he lived a fully human life. Jesus ate, slept, felt pain and joy and this is very important to Christians as it means God knows what our human experience is like.

JOHN 1:14 says that:

> "The Word became flesh and made his home among us."

Jesus is believed to be God's Word who lived on earth and who, through his death and resurrection, is able to bring God and humanity back into relationship again. God shows how much he loves the world by coming to earth and experiencing terrible suffering and death in order to pay the penalty for human sin. Christians believe that through the death and resurrection of Jesus all humanity can be forgiven and, after death, live eternally with God.

The belief that God came to earth in Jesus, (the Incarnation), to demonstrate his love and to save humanity is a very important and core belief of Christianity. In summary, it shows that God:

- **LOVES THE WORLD** - So much that he would come to earth and live a fully human life to show humanity how to live

- **UNDERSTANDS** - He understands what it is like to live as a human, experiencing the joys and pains of human existence. Philippians 2:6-7 says that though he was God, Jesus took the form of a servant

- **WAS WILLING** - He was willing to do something about the broken relationship between Him and humanity, which could not be repaired by humanity

- **GAVE HIS ONLY SON** - That God "loved the world so much that He gave his only begotten Son" (John 3:16), so that humanity could be forgiven and redeemed

A verse in the Bible that sums up Christian belief in the incarnation is from 1 Timothy Chapter 3, verse 16, which says:

"This Christian life is a great mystery, far exceeding our understanding, but some things are clear enough. Jesus appeared in a human body, was proved right by the invisible Spirit, was seen by angels. He was proclaimed by all kinds of peoples, believed in all over the world, taken up into heavenly glory."

For both the Creation and Incarnation sections, read John Chapter 1, verses 1 to 18. In these verses:

- Christ is described as God

- God created the world through Jesus

- God became fully human in Jesus and lived with humanity on earth. We can now see God in Jesus

- Jesus is full of grace and truth

THE PASSION OF CHRIST

The Passion of Christ refers to the last days of Christ on earth, and covers the events of the Last Supper, betrayal, arrest, trial, crucifixion, resurrection and ascension. These events are described in Luke Chapters 22-24, and are specifically remembered by Christians during Holy Week, which is the week before Easter.

The Last Supper took place when Jesus was together with his disciples and friends for a meal. During the meal, Jesus talked about how he soon would be leaving them, and would send them the Holy Spirit. He says that he is going to give his body for them, represented by bread, and that the wine represents the blood he will shed. Shortly after, Jesus suggests that he will be betrayed by someone sitting around the table. This person is **JUDAS**.

The meal becomes very important in Christian tradition as the foundation of the sacrament known as the **EUCHARIST** or **HOLY COMMUNION**, where Christians receive the bread and wine to remember the death of Christ and the sacrificing of his body and blood to save humanity from sin. The Eucharist is celebrated in most churches on a regular basis as it represents core beliefs of Christianity and demonstrates Christian understanding of who Jesus is and what he did.

Shortly after the meal, Jesus prays in a garden called **GETHSEMANE**, and is in great pain thinking about the death he is to face. This is important to Christians because it demonstrates how Jesus understands what it feels like to suffer. Following Judas' betrayal, Jesus is then arrested and found guilty of blasphemy by the Jewish religious leaders. The charge of blasphemy against Jesus is because he was believed to be claiming to be the Son of God, which was punishable by death. **PONTIUS PILATE**, the local Roman governor, sentences Jesus to death by crucifixion, which was a form of capital punishment.

Jesus is mocked and beaten and put on a cross, where he dies. The death of Jesus takes place on Friday, and the Christian Church now remembers the day as Good Friday. The use of the word "good" refers to the Christian belief that the death of Jesus was part of God's plan to bring salvation from sin, which is a good thing. Christians understand that through Jesus' suffering and death, people can receive forgiveness for the things they have done wrong against God and others. This also illustrates that Jesus is the rescuer or saviour promised in the Old Testament.

Three days later, in an event now celebrated on Easter Sunday, Christians believe Jesus rose from the dead. The resurrection is central to Christian belief and worship, because it demonstrates that Jesus is part of the Trinity as only God has the power to rise from the dead. It demonstrates that God is all powerful and that death is not the end and that, after death, people can be resurrected to eternal life now that their sins have been forgiven and they have been brought back to God. This belief of being brought back to God is known as atonement.

In Christian belief, 40 days after Jesus was resurrected, he ascended or went up to heaven. After his ascension, the Holy Spirit, whom Jesus had promised, came upon the disciples to enable them to spread the news of Jesus and live as Christians, putting their beliefs into action.

SALVATION AND ATONEMENT

In the Creation story of Genesis Chapter 2 God places a man and a woman in the Garden of Eden, with the explicit instructions not to eat from "the tree of the knowledge of good and evil." God says that if they eat of that tree they shall "surely die." In Genesis 3, Adam and Eve eat from the tree. As a result, the relationship between God and humans, which had been perfect, is broken, and this becomes known as The Fall. Adam and Eve "fall" from their position of closeness to God and are separated from God by sin, that is, their disobedience to God.

In the 4th Century Bishop Augustine, said that this was the story of **ORIGINAL SIN**. The first humans committed the original sin or act of disobedience to God and evil and suffering came into God's perfect world as a result of their actions. Many Christians believe that every human has inherited that sinful nature from the first humans and therefore will disobey God just like Adam and Eve did. This is a law that humans seem to be under - that, despite our best efforts, we will disobey God. Christians believe that the Old Testament commandments and law helped bring order to society, but did not bridge the gap between God and humans.

Because humans are separated from God by sin, something needs to be done to bring them back together again. It is obvious to Augustine that humans cannot do anything about bridging that gap as they have caused it in the first place. It is as if they need to be **BORN AGAIN**, which is a phrase some Christians use. Christians believe that because God is loving and kind, he has acted to restore the relationship between himself and humanity, by coming to earth in the form of Jesus, and making it possible for people to have a fresh start.

Jesus has sacrificed his life to pay the price for humans getting it wrong, and to redeem them. Redeeming something means to make it new again, or to restore it to the way it was. Jesus has made it possible for humans to have a relationship with God again because he has wiped out the consequences of sin. His perfect life and sacrifice has meant God and humans are "at one" again - he has given humanity the chance for **AT-ONE-MENT**. This gift of Jesus is a gift of God's grace to humanity - grace is where we are given something which we don't deserve or cannot get however much we try. Sometimes the death of Jesus is called a ransom, where a price is paid to set another person (humanity) free. It can also be seen as an image from a court of law where an innocent person (Jesus) takes the punishment for someone else who is guilty (humanity).

Because God has sacrificed his life for humanity, it is possible for humans to receive salvation, which is the forgiveness of sins, and eternal life. Humanity is able to be in a relationship with God again, through Christ's death, and then in his presence after death. We no longer have to be separated from God by sin. Jesus died for all humanity, but also rose from death to show that death is not final.

Many Christians say that it is only necessary for a Christian to believe in what Christ has done, and they will receive salvation, and be at one with God in this life and after death. Others believe that it is necessary for people to show that they are sorry for their sins and repent or turn away from them in order to receive Jesus' offer of salvation and be redeemed. Many Christians, particularly Roman Catholics, argue that we have to keep close to God and receive the sacraments, such as baptism and the Eucharist, to be sure of having salvation and eternal life.

The death and resurrection of Jesus, and the atonement, redemption and salvation that comes from them, are significant within Christianity. The act of Jesus rescuing humanity from original sin by sacrificing his life shows the love that God has for his world, as shown in John 3:10-21 and Acts 4:8-12. The belief that Christians can live in relationship with God again is very important, and, again, shows the work of the Trinity, as Christians believe it is the Holy Spirit who helps Christians access God the Father's grace, and then helps them to follow the teaching and example of Jesus in their lives.

CHRISTIAN ESCHATOLOGY

ESCHATOLOGY is the study of the **END TIMES** or what might happen at the end of the world. Christians believe that there will be a final judgement on all people at the end of time before a new era is brought in where God's kingdom is established.

- Based on teaching in Revelation 21, Christians believe that there will be a kingdom where there will be "no more tears or sadness" and any injustices will be corrected

- In this new era, God will dwell fully with his people, and the Church will be in union with Jesus, which is described as a marriage

- Many Christians believe that this era will take place on a renewed earth, where heaven and earth are properly united. This is based on teaching in Revelation 21:1 and Isaiah 65:17

- There are different understandings of what will take place before the new kingdom is established, with many Christians suggesting that there will be a persecution of anyone who calls themselves Christian. This is based on teaching in Luke 21:12-19

- As well as persecution, in Luke 21 Jesus says that there will be:

    - wars and uprisings
    - people claiming to be him
    - nation fighting nation
    - earthquakes, famine and disease
    - signs in the sun, moon and the stars

and it is at that time that people will see, "the Son of Man coming in a cloud with power and great glory."

The implications of this teaching are very important for Christians today:

- Because Christians believe that they will, alongside every other person, be judged for how they have lived; this gives importance to how they live now, including how they treat others and the decisions they make and their attitude towards the needy

- The belief that Jesus will come suddenly also makes Christians aware that they have to be ready at all times, living a life that pleases God

- This belief gives hope that earthquakes and terrible famines will not have the final word and there is a place with no more pain, sadness or injustice

Eschatology also concerns what happens after death and what will be revealed at that stage.

Christians believe that there is life after death, although there are different views about what precisely happens when a person dies. Because Jesus was resurrected, if people put their trust in him, then they too will receive new life after death, though not new life back on earth. Reincarnation is not a Christian belief.

Many Christians believe that, after death, although the body stays in the grave, the soul goes immediately to God for judgement. This belief is known as the immortality of the soul. Those who have trusted Jesus and received salvation and cleansing from sins due to the sacrifice of Jesus go to Heaven, where they will be for eternity in the presence of God, with no more pain or sadness. Those who have not trusted Jesus and have not received salvation will go to Hell. Hell is now viewed by many Christians as the absence of God rather than a place of eternal torment and punishment.

Other Christians believe in the resurrection of the body, which will take place at the end of time on Judgement Day when Jesus pronounces God's judgement on every person who has ever lived. At this time, some Christians believe that everyone will go to heaven, which is a theory called universalism, but others believe God will separate people into heaven and hell.

The primary reason for Christian belief in life after death is because of the resurrection of Jesus. Jesus also taught that there are:

- "many rooms in my Father's house which I am going to prepare" (John 14:2)

- He also said to the dying thief on the cross that, after his death, he would be in Paradise with Jesus that same day (Luke 23:43)

- Furthermore, he described himself as the "resurrection and the life", stating that, "he who believes in me will live, even though he dies" (John 11:25-6)

- Throughout history the church has taught that there is life after death and it is stated in both the Nicene and the Apostles Creeds, which are important statements of Christian beliefs

However, some Christians argue that, whilst belief in Christ is important, it is our actions that will be judged, as is shown in the parable of the sheep and the goats (Matthew 25), where the **SHEEP** (the righteous) are given eternal life based on the good deeds they have done rather than what beliefs they have.

- Other Christians do not believe a God of love would allow anyone to go to hell, or that there is such a place

- In contrast, others argue that because God is both loving and just there has to be a place where evil is punished

Roman Catholics believe that after a person dies, if they are in a "state of grace", their soul goes to a place called purgatory. Purgatory is not a place where God decides whether a soul should go to heaven or hell. It is a place where the soul of someone who has died already "in God's grace" is purified before entering heaven, as nothing unclean can enter the presence of God.

However, in 1563, when the beliefs of the Anglican Church (Church of England) were established following the break from the Catholic Church, The Thirty Nine Articles of Religion were developed. These articles form the basis of Anglican doctrine even today, and in Article 22, the Church of England rejected belief in purgatory, believing it has no basis in the Bible.

Orthodox, Roman Catholic and Protestant teaching argues that there are two judgements. The first one takes place at the time of our individual death, where Jesus judges our soul and we know what our final destiny will be. The second one, the Last Judgement, takes place at the end of the world and is a general judgement of all the nations. This is when Jesus will return to earth to raise the dead, which is called the **PAROUSIA**; in Catholic belief it is at this time that those in purgatory will go to Heaven.

Many Christians believe that, at this time when God raises and judges the dead, they will receive a new resurrected body. St. Paul writes about longing for:

> *"A heavenly body"*

in 2 Corinthians 5:1-10, a Bible passage which ends with the teaching that:

> *"All must appear before the judgement seat of Christ."*

Christians argue that belief in the existence of life after death for all people follows from Christ's own resurrection and his teaching. For Christians:

- **MAKE SENSE** - Belief in life after death helps make sense of this life, particularly when it is not fair, as everything will be fair and just in the end

- **PROVIDES PURPOSE** - In addition, this belief comforts people when they are facing bereavement and loss, and provides a purpose in life, knowing that the actions in this life will be judged and that there is something greater than this life, post death

THE PROBLEM OF EVIL AND SUFFERING

The problem of evil and suffering is a major challenge to Christian belief and raises the question:

> *"If God is all loving, why is there suffering, pain and evil in the world? Or, to put it another way, what does it say about the nature of God if there is evil and suffering in the world?"*

Early Greek philosopher **EPICURUS** put the problem of evil and suffering in the following form:

- Is God willing to prevent suffering, but not able?

- If so, then he is not omnipotent

- Is God able to prevent suffering, but not willing?

- If so, then he is malevolent (evil) and not omnibenevolent

- If God is both able and evil to prevent suffering, then why does it exist? If he is neither able nor willing, then why call him God?

This conundrum is sometimes called the **EPICUREAN PARADOX**.

In more recent times, **JL MACKIE** has reformulated the paradox into the form of three statements, known as The Inconsistent Triad. He argues that it is not possible for all three of the following statements to be true at the same time:

- **OMNIBENEVOLENT** - God is all good

- **OMNIPOTENT** - God is all powerful

- **EXISTING** - Evil exists

MACKIE says that if God has the two qualities listed above he would want to remove suffering, and he would have the power to do so. He concludes therefore that as evil does exist, obviously God does not. It is a logical contradiction to suggest that evil and suffering exist and an all good and all powerful God exists.Traditionally, evil and suffering is divided into two types:

- **HUMAN** - Suffering that is caused by humanity, for example, war, murder, torture, etc. is known as moral evil. It is given this name because the person or people who committed the act made a deliberate choice to carry out wrong

- **NATURAL** - Suffering that is caused by nature, for example, flooding, earthquakes, tsunamis, etc., is called natural evil. It is given this name because the suffering that results is caused by a natural process

However, natural events such as flooding, can be down to human actions such as deforestation or due to human-influenced climate change, so the distinction between the two types of evil is not straightforward. Similarly, illnesses such as cancer might be seen as a natural process in some cases, but caused by heavy smoking in others.

Both forms of evil, which cause immense suffering, are challenging to Christians, and have resulted in some Christians struggling to maintain their faith in the goodness of God. This can affect how Christians feel about God's goodness when they come to worship. Some Christians use Bible passages such as Psalm 103, which suggests God does care for humanity, and is a Father who can be trusted, even if things are not always easy and life is very fragile. The Psalm includes these verses:

> *"As a father has compassion on his children, so the Lord has compassion on those who fear him; for he knows how we are formed, he remembers that we are dust.*
>
> *The life of mortals is like grass,*
>
> *they flourish like a flower of the field;*
>
> *the wind blows over it and it is gone, and its place remembers it no more.*
>
> *But from everlasting to everlasting*
>
> *the Lord's love is with those who fear him.*
>
> *The Lord works righteousness*
>
> *and justice for all the oppressed."*

CHRISTIAN RESPONSES TO THE PROBLEM OF EVIL AND SUFFERING

Christian responses to the problem of evil and suffering and the challenges it raises about the nature of God, can be divided into three main areas:

Responses from the Bible

Many of the Psalms in the Old Testament are honest songs about how people seem to suffer, but, in those times of suffering, God has not forgotten or abandoned them. In Psalm 119, the writer says that his:

> "Soul is weary with sorrow"

but asks God to:

> "Strengthen me with your word."

He goes on to write about how, if a person keeps God's law and resists evil, he will be **DELIVERED** and **PRESERVED**. Even though he says that "the wicked set a trap for me," and asks to be, "redeemed from human oppression," he feels that "the Lord is near" and that "there is peace for those who follow His Law."

The Psalms are very honest, and recognise human pain. In Psalm 119, the author cries out to God, "when will you comfort me?", but, ultimately, clings on to his faith in God. Psalms and other passages like this give Christians great hope that not only does God hear their prayers, but that he will deliver them from their suffering, even if that is not until after death.

One person in the **OLD TESTAMENT** who experienced terrible suffering was a man named **JOB**.

- Although he is a good man with enormous wealth, who is praised by God for his righteousness, God allows Satan to test him. In the Bible, Satan, or the Devil, is present on many occasions, and is seen as a fallen angel who works against God. The testing of Job involves taking his children and many flocks and causing him great pain with body sores and mental torment

- Although advised to admit that he has done something to deserve his suffering, Job responds by saying that he is innocent. In Job 3, he curses the day he is born, and says that "he has no rest, only turmoil." Throughout the book, where the advice of his friends is of no use, Job clings on to the fact that, somehow, "to God belong wisdom and power."

- At the end of the book, we hear God's voice. He does not defend himself, but suggests that humans have little idea of how omnipotent he is as a Creator of all things and the giver of all life. Job responds by saying that God is way beyond anything he could possibly understand

Christians learn from this that:

- God allows things to happen which are very difficult for us to understand. Because of this there are no easy solutions to why evil is in the world

- Suffering seems to be part of life both for people who try to follow God and those who don't

- Job recognises that these things do not change the nature and character of God as righteous, omnipotent and omniscient

The greatest help from the Bible for when Christians experience evil and suffering is the example of Jesus. As Christians believe that Jesus was God in human form, they believe that God knows what it is like to feel pain, sorrow and anguish. There are times in the New Testament when Jesus is recorded as:

- Deeply distressed when a friend dies (John 11:33)

- In great agony when he knows his own death is near (Luke 22:44)

The belief that God experienced great pain gives comfort to Christians during difficult times, and helps them in worship, as it reminds Christians that God knows about human experience, with all its joys and pains. The death and resurrection of Jesus gives Christians hope that suffering and death is not the end, but that there is a better after life in Heaven, where there will be no more tears, pain or suffering.

Responses in Christian belief

One major Christian response to the problem of evil and suffering is to believe that humans have free will, which was first given to Adam and Eve. Humans are not forced to make good choices, which means that some choices we make are not wise and result in suffering. However, to have free will is a good thing, and can result in good choices, such as freely choosing to love someone. Christians believe that God shows his goodness in giving humanity freedom to choose, as it allows us to live fully, make mistakes and learn from them, and not live like robots.

Another Christian response is to believe that this life on earth is a time for our souls to develop. Irenaeus, an early Christian teacher, believed that this life was a way of shaping our souls so that every experience of life, even the painful ones, helps us to develop and grow closer to God. This theory sometimes calls life a vale of soul-making. Although we pass through a vale (valley) and at times it is dark, if we learn the lessons in those times, then the journey shapes our souls to develop characteristics such as patience, compassion and empathy.

Practical Christian responses to suffering & evil

- Christians believe that one of the most important ways to respond to evil and suffering is to show the love of God by caring for others
- Christian charities, such as World Vision, The Salvation Army and CAFOD (Catholic Agency for Overseas Development) help millions of people who are experiencing the consequences of natural disaster, poverty, war and other events that have resulted in suffering
- On a local level, many Christians choose to work in caring professions, such as nursing or social care, or help out in their communities by visiting the elderly or working with the homeless
- Many Christians regularly support relief efforts by raising or giving money
- A second practical response is for Christians to pray for others and the world. Many Christians pray that God will comfort those who are in pain and suffering, and that peace will come to areas which are in conflict. Other Christians, particularly those from the Charismatic churches, will pray directly for people, that God will heal them

ARE CHRISTIAN RESPONSES TO SUFFERING & EVIL SUCCESSFUL OR CONVINCING?

Responses from the Bible

- Many Christians find comfort and hope from the Bible, and sections such as the Psalms and Job, and the belief that God knows about their suffering and pain. They are supported by the idea that, as seen in the life of Jesus, God knows what pain is like

- However, this does not stop the fact that there is suffering and pain, so why doesn't God stop it? Christians might wonder if God can actually stop it

- It might also make Christians wonder why God made a world in which enormous evil and suffering takes place

Responses in Christian belief

- Because of free will, Christians believe that humanity is responsible for much of the suffering that goes on in the world

- Free will is a good thing, even though the consequences of that free will might result in evil and suffering, and things such as murder and war. Free will also results in kindness and compassion

- However, God is omniscient so must have known that humanity would abuse the gift of free will, so is it God's fault that suffering takes place?

- It could be argued that learning our lessons from suffering so that our soul develops is a very painful way of growth and development - perhaps too painful for many people

■ Practical Christian responses to suffering and evil

- Christians do not believe that prayer and charity will stop suffering. These are practical ways in which they can show the love of God and compassion for others

- However, many atheists might suggest that it is strange to pray to God to stop suffering when he is the one who allowed it in the first place

- Christians might respond by arguing that at a time of suffering and loss, people do not want a set of explanations about why they are suffering, and why God does or does not seem to answer prayer, but to know someone is there caring for them and helping them get things back together again, if possible

Marriage & the Family

Area of Study 1 - Marriage & the Family

KEYWORDS

- **ANNULMENT** - A declaration by the Church that a marriage can be ended because it was not lawful or true

- **ATHEIST** - A person who does not believe that God or Gods exist

- **BLENDED FAMILY** - A family unit made up of a married couple and their children, including a child or children from a previous marriage/s

- **CIVIL PARTNERSHIP** - A legal relationship between two people of the same sex that gives them the same rights as a married couple

- **COHABITATION** - Living together without being married

- **CONTRACEPTION** - The deliberate use of artificial methods or other techniques to prevent pregnancy from occurring

- **DIVORCE** - The formal ending of a marriage by a legal process

- **EXTENDED FAMILY** - A nuclear family and their close relatives, such as the children's grandparents, aunts and uncles living together

- **FAMILY PLANNING** - Planning how many children to have in a relationship and when

- **HOMOSEXUALITY** - Sexual attraction to a person of the same sex

- **HUMANAE VITAE** - 1968 document from the Pope guiding Roman Catholics about family life and procreation

- **HUMANISM** - A system of values that emphasises the value of human beings, and which prefers critical reasoning to religion

- **MARRIAGE** - A legally accepted union between two people as partners in a relationship

- **NUCLEAR FAMILY** - A couple and their children, living together as a unit

- **PARISH** - An area cared for by a priest and the local church

- **PRE-MARITAL SEX** - Sex before marriage
- **PROCREATION** - Making a new life
- **REMARRIAGE** - Marrying again after a previous marriage ends
- **RITE OF PASSAGE** - A ceremony or event to mark an important stage in someone's life, eg the transition from childhood to adulthood
- **SAME SEX MARRIAGE** - Legally accepted union between two people of the same sex as partners in a relationship
- **SINGLE PARENT FAMILY** - A lone parent and dependent child/children living as a family unit
- **SITUATION ETHICS** - A method of trying to do the most loving thing in each situation

MARRIAGE

Within Christianity, marriage is regarded as very significant. Emphasis is placed on the role that committed and faithful marriages make to stable family life and society.

Marriage is supported in the Bible and Christian teaching:

- **UNITED INTO ONE** - In Genesis 2:24, at the beginning of creation, the man and woman are joined to each other, and "united into one." Many Christians think that this signifies the importance that God places on marriage, as this verse comes at the very beginning of the Bible and God's plan for humanity
- **GENESIS** - In his own teaching about marriage in Mark 10:6-9 Jesus repeats the verse from Genesis to stress the importance and central role of marriage
- **HOLY** - Marriage is regarded by many Christians as a sacrament, which is an occasion or event where God gives his grace. This highlights the sanctity of marriage, where the relationship is regarded as holy, meaning that it is something to be kept pure and honouring to God

In Hebrews 13:4, the author writes:

"Let marriage be held in honour among all, and let the marriage bed be undefiled, for God will judge the sexually immoral and adulterous."

- **SEXUAL RELATIONSHIPS** - For many Christians, marriage is the only appropriate setting for sexual relationships, as the sexual intimacy takes place within a committed partnership already blessed by God. Christians believe God is love and wants people to give and receive love, which is what happens in marriage

- **PURPOSE** - Protestant Christianity has emphasised that the role and purpose of marriage is to bring comfort and joy to each of the partners, and stability in society. In Protestant and Catholic Churches it is also the relationship God has designed for the purpose of procreation and family life. For all Christians, marriage is intended to last until the death of one of the spouses

- **HETEROSEXUAL** - Traditional Christian teaching regards marriage to be between one man and one woman

However, **ATHEIST** and **HUMANIST** attitudes challenge the need to place such emphasis on marriage. In the past 50 years society has changed, meaning that in the 21st Century people should be free to enter relationships which involve different types of family life:

- **CHOICE** - People should be free to choose whether to have children without necessarily being in a long-term relationship to the father or mother of the child

- **ANY RELATIONSHIP** - People should be free to raise children in a variety of settings. This could be within a cohabiting partnership, same sex relationship or as a single parent who has chosen to raise children without a partner. Marriage is no longer as important for fulfilling this purpose

- **NO PRESSURE** - There should be no pressure for people to make a commitment to marriage, and some atheists and humanists argue that the promise "until death us do part" is unrealistic. All that matters is that humans treat each other with respect in their relationships and look out for each other's good

In response, whilst believing marriage is still vitally important, some Christians, in denominations such as the Methodist Church, teach that a long-term, stable and committed relationship can be an appropriate setting for sexual relationships and family life. The Church of England no longer calls living together before marriage as **LIVING IN SIN**, whilst the Roman Catholic Church will marry people who have been living together and have children before marriage, as long as those to be married are part of the Catholic Church. The United Reformed Church now allows its priests to conduct same sex marriages.

Christian teaching still emphasises that marriage is the primary setting for stable family life, which God intends for the welfare of children and society.

SEXUAL RELATIONSHIPS

Marriage and sex

Christians teach that sex should be loving and a sign of **COMMITMENT**, and should take place within marriage, to bring unity and joy to the couple and for procreation:

- **NOT SHAMEFUL** - God instructed Adam and Eve to be "fruitful and multiply", so sex is not seen as dirty or unclean

- **EXPRESSION OF LOVE** - Christians teach God's plan for sex is that it is an expression of love within marriage between two faithful partners

- **NO SEX WITHOUT MARRIAGE** - As well as being an expression of a loving marriage, the potential outcome of sex is so significant that pre-marital sex or adultery is not God's plan for sex

- **NO PROMISCUITY** - All Christians disapprove of promiscuity

- **CONSIDER MARRIAGE** - Some Christians argue that a long-term, stable and committed relationship can be a fitting setting for sexual relationships, but would encourage the partners to consider marriage. Others, however, believe that all sex outside marriage, even if the partners intend to get married, is wrong

Christian attitudes towards homosexuality

Some Christians believe that homosexuality is wrong because:

- **AGAINST GOD'S PLAN** - It goes against God's plan for sexual relationships and marriage, which should be between one woman and one man

- **NO CHILDREN** - Homosexual relationships cannot naturally procreate, which Christians believe is a core purpose of marriage

- **CONDEMNED** - It is condemned in the Bible, which states that men who did not honour God, "abandoned the natural function for that which is unnatural" and, "men with men committed indecent acts" for which they "received due penalty" (Romans 1:21, 26-27)

Some Christians believe that the teaching of 1 Corinthians 6:9 applies today. In that verse, homosexuality is included in a list of actions that exclude people from the Kingdom of God. In verses 18 and 19 of the same chapter, Christians are encouraged to **FLEE IMMORALITY** (wrong actions) as their "body is a temple of the Holy Spirit."

Some Christians believe that these verses are still a source of authority for today, and that they disallow any sexual relationships outside heterosexual marriage.

However, other Christians argue that:

- **NATURAL** - Homosexuality is natural and people should be allowed to express their sexuality

- **LOVE** - God is a God of love, so celebrates love wherever it is shown

- **EQUALITY** - Everyone is born in the image of God, and equal, so should be shown respect

- **NO DISCRIMINATION** - Jesus said that we should love one another without discrimination

- **TEACHING** - Teaching on homosexuality should be changed to reflect changing attitudes in the UK

Atheist and Humanist views

Atheists and Humanists argue that people should be free to express their sexuality in different ways, as long as it does not hurt the other person or persons involved.

- **RESPECT** - A person's sexuality should be respected

- **EQUALITY** - People should be allowed equal access to legal rights, such as marriage

- **OUTDATED** - The Church's teaching is outdated and based on belief in a supernatural deity and religious dogma, not reasoned argument

- **FAIRNESS** - In the 21st Century, discrimination on the grounds of sexuality has no place

Mixed views and responses in different churches

- **CHURCH OF ENGLAND** - Same sex marriage is not allowed, and same sex relationships are not blessed. Permission is given for priests and Bishops to enter into a civil partnership as long as the relationship is celibate

- **METHODIST CHURCH** - Considering whether to allow same sex marriage, whilst the United Reformed Church has decided to let its local churches decide if they want to conduct same sex marriages

- **ROMAN CATHOLIC CHURCH** - Does not allow for same sex marriages or bless same sex unions. Homosexual desires are not sinful, but are if they are acted out. It argues that homosexual people should be given respect and care, but that homosexual behaviour is against God's law, which does not change

- **QUAKERS** - Argue that to reject people because of their sexual behaviour is a denial of God's creation, and accept homosexual relationships

CHRISTIAN TEACHING ON MARRIAGE AND FAMILY LIFE

All Christians believe that the family is very significant because it is:

- **BUILDING BLOCK** - The basic building block that God has designed for the welfare of society
- **PROCREATION** - The best place for procreation, and a safe environment for the growth and development of children
- **RIGHT/WRONG** - The place where children receive teaching about right and wrong
- **DEMONSTRATION** - Where children see Christian values, beliefs and practices demonstrated
- **VIRTUES** - The place where virtues such as patience, kindness and compassion can be developed
- **VULNERABILITY** - The place where the safety and welfare of vulnerable, young and old members of the family can be lovingly assured

The reason Christians believe the family is important is because the Bible and the teaching of the Church stress the significant role it plays.

The Bible

In Ephesians 6:1-4, the relationship between children and parents is outlined as one which should be mutually respectful. Children are taught to **HONOUR THEIR MOTHER AND FATHER**.

Fathers are instructed not to:

> "Provoke their children to anger by the way they treat them."

Rather, fathers are told to:

> "Bring children up with discipline and instruction that comes from the Lord."

The verses go on to say that the honouring of parents results in a long life, and that things will go well for those who follow God's teaching in the family home.

The Church of England

The CoE stresses that marriage is for the joy and comfort of the partners in it, and for the joy of children. It teaches that:

> *"Children thrive, grow and develop within the love and safeguarding of a family. Within the family we care for the young, the old and those with needs. Families offer commitment, fun, love, companionship and security."*

The Roman Catholic Church teaches that the family is blessed by God as the union which results in new life through procreation. In the Catechism (Catholic Church teaching) it notes that:

> *"The family is the community in which, from childhood, one can learn moral values, begin to honour God and make good use of freedom."*

Many Christians regard the **TRADITIONAL NUCLEAR FAMILY** as God's design for family life. However, attitudes towards family life have changed within society and are changing within the Church.

SUPPORT FOR THE FAMILY IN THE LOCAL PARISH

Recognising that there are many models of family life in the 21st Century, such as single parent, cohabiting parents with children, same-sex marriages, extended and blended, the Church, through its work in local parishes, attempts to support families and parents through:

- **WELCOME** - Offering welcome and support to all parents through weekly parent and toddler groups
- **GUIDANCE** - Offering parenting and marriage guidance classes
- **EDUCATION** - Providing Christian education on marriage and family life through schools, where the local priest will often visit and be on the board of governors
- **FAMILY SERVICES** - Holding family services in the local church on special occasions such as at Easter and Christmas

- **CEREMONIES** - Offering to conduct ceremonies which mark rites of passage. These rites of passage, such as baptism, confirmation and marriage are outlined by the local priest when he meets the family and explains Christian beliefs and teachings and the significance of the step being taken

All churches stress that the parish consists of everyone in a geographical area, and not just those who attend church. This is based on Jesus' teaching that Christians should love their neighbours and that everyone is their neighbour.

Christians attempt to do this whilst still trying to uphold Christian teaching on the sanctity of marriage, sexual relationships and family life, and therefore might encourage cohabiting parents to consider marriage.

The Church recognises that one of the most vulnerable groups in society is children.

In Matthew 19:13-14 Jesus teaches that children should not be discouraged or forbidden from meeting him, even though the followers of Jesus at the time thought he would be too busy for them. Because of this, the Christian church organises:

- **SUNDAY SCHOOL** - Classes especially for children
- **FAMILY WORSHIP SERVICES** - That include children
- **SPECIAL EVENTS** - For children and young people such as: Soul Survivor, and Warrior Camps, where emphasis is placed on relevant worship and teaching about central aspects of Christian belief and practice

National Christian organisations that attempt to support and encourage the welfare of marriage and family life include:

- **CATHOLIC CARE** - Provides a team of social workers specialising in family care, who deliver practical support to children, young people and their families, regardless of the particular family structure those young people are in
- **CARE FOR THE FAMILY** - Which is committed to:

    "Strengthening family life and helping those who are hurting because of family difficulties ... bringing hope and compassion."

- **THE CATHOLIC MARRIAGE ADVISORY SERVICE**
- **THE METHODIST HOMES FOR THE AGED**
- **THE CHILDREN'S SOCIETY**

Whilst the traditional Christian family model is not to live in extended families, Christians are taught to care for their parents as they become more vulnerable, and may use the services above or care for them locally with the support of the parish.

FAMILY PLANNING AND BIRTH CONTROL

There are different attitudes within Christianity towards using artificial methods of contraception:

Sacred Union

The Roman Catholic belief is that sex expresses a sacred union between a man and a woman. Through this act of love, God brings about new life, and nothing should interfere with God's creative act. Therefore, every time a married couple have sexual intercourse, there should be the possibility of new life being created and no artificial contraception should be used. Procreation is a core purpose of marriage.

Pro-Life

Catholic teaching is pro-life, and is informed by documents such as Humanae Vitae, which outlined teaching on marriage, responsible parenting and the regulation of birth. The teaching stressed that man is:

> *"Not free to act as they choose in the service of transmitting life ... but bound to ensure that what they do corresponds to the will of God the Creator."*

> *"Every marital act [of sex] must retain its intrinsic relationship to the procreation of human life."*

> *"The direct interruption [ie artificial contraception] of the generative process ... is to be absolutely excluded as a lawful means of regulating the number of children."*

Humanae Vitae

This means that man cannot **PLAY GOD** or go against God's natural law in deciding when a child is conceived, but must allow for that possibility every time sex takes place.

The teaching of **HUMANAE VITAE** allows for a husband and wife to "space out" when they have their children by having intercourse during those times when a woman is less likely to conceive. This is a natural method of contraception.

Humanae Vitae warned that use of artificial birth control would result in an increase in casual sex, without mutual love and respect for procreation, and this would undermine family life.

Some Evangelical Christians support the above view, believing that it is God and not man who decides if sexual intercourse results in pregnancy.

Many Protestant groups believe that the act of sex is also to bring unity and joy in marriage and does not always have to be for the purpose of procreation. They allow artificial contraception to be used, such as condoms or the pill, which prevents a pregnancy from commencing.

In addition to enabling them to plan a family, in times of illness, financial difficulty or stress, or if a pregnancy might be harmful to the mother or family, a couple should still have the possibility of sexual joy and therefore could use contraception.

Most Christians believe that once a pregnancy has begun it should be carried through to full term, and therefore, whilst they might support artificial contraception that prevents sperm meeting egg, they would disagree with contraceptives such as the morning after pill, or using abortion as a form of contraception.

Situation Ethics

Some Christians believe Christ taught that doing the most loving thing in every situation is what is important. This is known as Situation Ethics:

- **AGAPE LOVE** - The love to be shown to others is known as agape love and tries to promote the best outcome for another person. This love avoids people doing what they think is the most loving thing just for them, and is an unselfish love

- **CONTRACEPTION IS LOVING** - If the most loving thing for a couple is to express their love for each other in sex, but they are not ready for a child or they already have many children, or it could be dangerous for the woman to get pregnant, then the most loving, (agape) thing to do could be to use artificial contraception

- **SHOULD GOD DECIDE?** - Roman Catholic teaching has criticised Situation Ethics as allowing human beings to become God in deciding what is loving and what is not

- **SEX & PROCREATION** - Catholics argue that God has already laid down a moral law that will result in the most benefit for human beings, and should be followed. Sex should not be separated from procreation

- **UNFORSEEN CONSEQUENCES** - Actions, even if loving, should not be decided in each situation, as this could result in unforeseen and unwanted consequences

- **GOD OF LOVE** - Jesus did not say that Christians should decide in each situation to do the most loving thing, but follow a God of love. Jesus, and teaching in the Bible, upholds the sanctity of marriage as the place of sexual intercourse and family life

Atheist and Humanist Responses

Most atheists and humanists do not object to artificial contraception, stressing the need for the child to be wanted and loved. This is because:

- **NO NATURAL LAW** - God has not laid down any laws for procreation and contraception

- **RESPONSIBLE ADULTS** - The decision to have children is therefore up to the people who have sexual intercourse

- **REASONED CONTROL** - The important thing is not following any religious law but allowing people to exercise reasoned control over their decisions

Atheist and humanist responses stress the right of the couple to choose when and if to have children and when to start a family in a responsible approach to sex and family life. In the 19th Century, humanist **JOHN STUART MILL** promoted birth control as a responsible approach towards sex. The approach would support human freedom and not the need to follow a Deity or Divine Law.

Humanists and atheists **DISAGREE** with the Roman Catholic Church as they allow artificial contraception to be used when one or more of the couple carry genetic disorders or conditions that could be passed on through sex. They would also agree with the use of birth control by artificial contraception if a person wants to have sex but is too young or not ready to have a child.

DIVORCE AND REMARRIAGE

In data from the Office for National Statistics, (2013), 42% of marriages **END IN DIVORCE**, which is the lowest rate of divorce for 40 years.

There are different attitudes within Christianity towards divorce and remarriage:

- **SACRAMENT** - Many Protestant Christians recognise marriage as a sacrament, where God's grace is given. Solemn promises are made to each other and the couple have every intention of keeping those promises

- **BROKEN PROMISES** - However, sometimes promises are broken through things such as adultery or unreasonable behaviour. In such cases, many churches offer counselling and attempt to help the couple reconcile their differences. If this cannot happen, and the marriage is irretrievably broken, then the Church of England and other Protestant Churches allow a couple to divorce. Sometimes, allowing a harmful marriage to end can be the lesser of two evils

- **REMARRIAGE** - If, after careful marriage preparation, the partners from a divorce wish to marry again (either each other, or another partner), then, in exceptional circumstances and on a case by case basis, decided by the local priest, remarriage in a Protestant Church is permitted. Prince Charles and Camilla Parker Bowles were not permitted to marry in church as adultery had led to the breakup of Charles' first marriage to Princess Diana

- **UNFAITHFULNESS** - Protestant Churches believe that Jesus allowed for divorce in the case of one partner being unfaithful. In Matthew 9 Jesus says that God allows divorce in this circumstance because people are "hard hearted" and don't live up to God's original intention for marriage. God is loving and forgiving if people do genuinely regret their actions

Roman Catholic attitudes towards divorce and remarriage are different

Following careful preparation by the priest, marriage in the Catholic Church is entered into as the lifelong union of the partners and God in a sacrament where God is present by his grace.

Marriage is therefore both a legal and spiritual bond. Because God is joined to the couple in a spiritual bond, a legal ceremony cannot break it, and therefore divorce is not allowed. In technical language:

> *"The Church does not recognise a civil divorce because the State cannot dissolve what is indissoluble."*

The Catholic Church accepts Jesus' teaching in Matthew 19:6, which states that:

> *"What God has joined together, let no one separate."*

In addition, St. Paul says in 1 Corinthians 7:10 that:

> *"The wife should not separate from her husband ... and the husband should not divorce his wife."*

Divorce attempts to break promises made with God and separate **ONE FLESH**, which is not possible. What is permitted, after serious questioning and a long time, is for a marriage to be annulled. This is where a marriage is ended because it was never true or lawful in the first place:

- **MENTAL INCAPACITY** - One partner was mentally unable to understand their vows
- **FORCED MARRIAGE** - One partner was forced into the marriage
- **NO CHILDREN** - One partner didn't intend to have children
- **NO CONSUMMATION** - The marriage has not been consummated
- **ANNULMENT** - An annulment is not a divorce. Following the annulment of the marriage by the Catholic Church, the couple must also get a civil (legal) divorce

- **DIVORCE NOT RECOGNISED** - Divorced people who have not had their marriage annulled cannot be remarried in a Catholic Church. Because divorce is not recognised, the Church regards the person as married and adultery would take place if they married again
- **WIDOWHOOD** - If a person's original marriage has not been annulled, the person can only be remarried if their original spouse has died

Non-religious approaches to marriage and divorce

Some people do not want to make promises before God in a Church on their wedding day, as that would go against their beliefs.

Humanist Weddings

HUMANIST weddings ceremonies can include readings, music, a symbolic ritual and the sharing of vows chosen by the couple, but have no reference or promises made to a God. Humanist weddings are not legally binding in England, and therefore the couple have to carry out legal requirements at a registry office. Though both humanists and atheists accept the seriousness of the commitments made in marriage, it is not regarded as sacred and therefore divorce is permitted. This is better than an unhappy and painful relationship.

Situation Ethics

The approach to marriage and divorce within Situation Ethics is based around the law of love. Nothing, like marriage or divorce, is labelled "good" or "bad" by itself. A marriage or divorce is only good if it demonstrates **AGAPE LOVE**.

The mature person asks what is the most loving action in each situation.

Situation Ethicists suggest that Jesus' teaching allows for divorce as he wants the most loving thing in each situation.

Love is the only thing that is always good, not rules or traditions, and therefore divorce is allowed where it is the most loving thing.

Christian Responses to Humanists

Christians respond to atheist and humanist approaches to marriage by suggesting that God is the source of all love, so to not make any reference to God in a marriage service misses out the foundation of all love and happiness, and does not offer the support that God and the Church can bring to a relationship.

Many Christians would agree that love is the most important thing in every situation. However, many would feel uncomfortable with what really motivates the ending of a marriage, and whether it really is the most loving thing to do, or if there are other less admirable motives. Many Christians regard Situation Ethics as disrespectful to the unchanging laws laid out in the Bible and have concerns about the power it gives to humans to decide whether or not to follow those laws.

THE EQUALITY OF MEN AND WOMEN IN THE FAMILY

Christians regard men and women as equal due to the teaching in Genesis when God created the first man and woman. GENESIS 1:27, says that God:

"Created humankind in his image; in the image of God he created them; male and female he created them."

As this is part of the first chapter of the Bible, many Christians think that this means that God's plan is for men and women to be equal as they are both made in his image.

For some Christians this means that all roles should be open equally to men and women, including roles within the family. Christians who take this stance suggest that Bible teaching such as Ephesians 5:22-24 should be read very carefully. The verses say:

"Wives, be subject to your husbands as you are to the Lord. For the husband is head of the wife just as Christ is head of the church. Just as the church is subject to Christ, so also wives ought to be, in everything, to their husbands."

Some Christians argue that if these verses are taken without the next verse, the teaching would place women under the authority of their husbands. In verse 25, the passage goes on to say:

> "Husbands, love your wives, just as Christ loved the church and gave himself up for her."

With this verse added, many Christians argue that it actually teaches that marriage is about mutual service, as a husband is willing to give his life for his wife and serve her in the same way Christ sacrificially served the church.

Christians who take this stance argue that this allows Church teaching to be in line with what takes place in 21st Century society where men and women can have equal roles in the family, are both able to go out to work and have careers, and have equal responsibility for the care of their children.

Other Christians, particularly within some Evangelical and Baptist Churches, regard the primary responsibility of woman as caring for the home and family.

Some Christians support this view with different verses from the Creation story, where, after the Fall, God says to Eve that:

> "Your desire shall be for your husband, and he shall rule over you."

1 Timothy 2:13-14 says that,

> "Adam was formed first, then Eve; and Adam was not deceived, but the woman was deceived and became a transgressor" (sinner)

These teachings are used to suggest an order in the family where the man is the head of the house and wage earner, and women have the role of serving the house and family. For many years, this was the traditional role of men and women in a Christian family. Whilst men and women in this view are regarded as equal before God, they are given different roles according to God's plan for family life.

In response, many Christians recognise that throughout history the teaching that Eve was the one who was weak and gave in to sin has caused much distress and accusations that Church teaching discriminates against women. For many Christians today, the Fall is a symbolic story of how all people fall short of God's standard, but can still share in God's love.

Area of Study 1 - Marriage & the Family

EQUALITY means that men and women have both equal opportunities and responsibilities in family life. Many Christians value the freedom of choice, arguing that if a partner chooses to be at home to care for the family, this is just as worthy as a career.

Describing family life, Pope John Paul II wrote that:

> *"All members of the family, each according to his or her own gift, have the grace and responsibility of building day by day the community of persons making a family a school of deeper humanity."*

St Paul, in 1 Corinthians 7:3, taught that both partners have equal responsibilities so that:

> *"The husband should please his wife as a husband. The wife should please her husband as a wife"*

Many Christians regard these teachings from the Bible and leaders of the Church as supporting total equality in the roles between men and women in the family setting.

CHRISTIAN TEACHING ABOUT GENDER PREJUDICE AND DISCRIMINATION

Christians are against gender prejudice and discrimination. **GALATIANS** 3:23-29 teaches that:

> *"You are now children of God because you trust in Christ. God does not see you as a Jew or as a Greek. He does not see you as a servant or a person free to work. He does not see you as a man or as a woman. You are all one in Christ."*

Christians try to follow this teaching and the example of Jesus, who treated women with great respect, going against many conventions of his culture and the way his own society regarded women. He gave dignity to women when they were not normally considered an important part of society.

Examples from history of Christian opposition to gender prejudice and discrimination:

- **WOLLSTONECRAFT** - In 1792, Mary Wollstonecraft published **A VINDICATION OF THE RIGHTS OF WOMEN**, arguing for the equal education of women. This was a radical thing to do at the time. Although she rejected much traditional teaching of the Church, she was motivated to write for better rights for women because of her belief that God had created men and women equal

- **SUFFRAGETTES** - Although the Church of England did not officially support the movement to get women the vote, the **CHURCH LEAGUE FOR WOMEN'S SUFFRAGE** and the **CATHOLIC WOMEN'S SUFFRAGE LEAGUE** had over 5,000 members in 1914. Many suffragettes used reasons from the Bible to support their cause

- **GLOBAL INEQUALITY** - Across the world Christian Aid is working to challenge gender norms and power structures, which it argues are a major factor in the continuing inequality between men and women. This inequality fails girls and women and stops them from reaching their potential

- **ROLE OF WOMEN** - Christians support equality but disagree about the role of women in the Church

- **WOMEN PRIESTS** - Many Protestant Churches, such as The Church of England, Methodist and The Salvation Army ordain women as priests. From 1986 to 1993, the leader of The Salvation Army was a female Officer (priest). In 2015, The Church of England appointed its **FIRST FEMALE BISHOP**. However, the Roman Catholic Church does not ordain women. There are several areas of disagreement between churches on the question of the ordination of women

Religion, Peace & Conflict

(3RB0/2A-2G)

Islamic Beliefs

Crime & Punishment

From an Islamic perspective

Area of Study 2 - Islamic Beliefs

KEYWORDS

- **ADALAT** - The justice of Allah; Divine justice (also known as 'Al-Adl')

- **AHL AL-BAYT** - Literally, "people of the house", the family of the prophet Muhammad

- **AKHIRAH** - The afterlife

- **ALLAH** - The Arabic name for God

- **AL-QADR** - Predestination

- **BARZAKH** - Literally "a veil" between two things; the period between a person's death and their resurrection on the Day of resurrection

- **BENEFICENCE** - Kindness, loving generosity

- **HADITH** - Records of the sayings and actions of Muhammad

- **IMAMAH** - The successors to Muhammad, disputed between Shi'a and Sunni Muslims

- **IMMANENCE** - The belief that Allah is present everywhere in the world and acts in it

- **INJIL** - Arabic name for the original Gospel of Isa (Jesus) revealed by Allah; one of four holy books of Scripture

- **KHALIFAH** - The religious and civic leader of a Muslim state (Caliphate) who represents Allah on earth

- **KITAB AL-IMAN** - The Book of Faith written in the 13th Century explaining the nature of Muslim life; part of the Hadith

- **KUTUB** - Muslim holy books, or books of Allah (Kutuballah)

- **MALAIKAH** - Arabic name for angels; spiritual beings who perform tasks given to them by Allah

- **MI'AD** - The belief that Allah will resurrect all of mankind to be judged

- **MIRACLE** - An event that is not able to be explained by natural or scientific laws, and which is attributed to Allah's actions

- **NUBUWWAH** - "Prophethood"; the principle that Allah has appointed prophets to teach his will to humanity

- **OMNIPOTENT** - All powerful

- **OMNISCIENT** - All knowing

- **PROPHET** - A person who is chosen to reveal Allah's guidance, correction and teachings to humanity

- **QUR'AN** - Revelation from Allah and the holiest and central religious text in Islam

- **RESURRECTION** - The concept of coming back to life after death; raised by Allah to life after death

- **REVELATION** - A divine or supernatural disclosure to humans of something about the nature of Allah and/or his purposes

- **RISALAH** - Arabic for "message". Allah's way of communicating to humanity through the prophets

- **SAHIFAH** - Literally, "page"; the scrolls of Ibrahim (Abraham) and Musa (Moses)

- **SCRIPTURE** - Holy book/text given or revealed to humanity by Allah through a prophet

- **SHI'A** - Muslims who believe that leadership of Islam should stay within Muhammad's own family (the ahl al-bayt)

- **SIN** - Anything that goes against Allah's law or will

- **SUNNI** - Muslims who believe that the successor to Muhammad, Abu Bakr (Muhammad's father-in-law) was the first of four 'rightly guided' leaders, elected by the Muslim community, though of no blood relation to Muhammad

- **SURAH** - A chapter of the Qur'an

- **TAWHID** - The essential Muslim belief that Allah is one, without equal and unique (monotheism)

- **TAWRAT** - Arabic word for the Torah; Muslims believe it is a holy book of Islam revealed by Allah to the prophet Musa (Moses)

- **TRANSCENDENCE** - The belief that Allah is separate from, and above and beyond, the universe

- **'USUL AD-DIN** - The five principles or roots of Shi'a Islam based on the Qur'an and Hadith, which Shi'a Muslims must follow

- **ZABUR** - The holy book revealed to the prophet Dawud (David); Psalms of David

THE SIX BELIEFS

There are two main groups (or denominations) in Islam, **SUNNI** and **SHI'A**, which hold many similar beliefs, but differ in some. Sunni and Shia Islam split following the death of Muhammad, the Final Prophet of Islam, in 632CE. Whilst Sunni Muslims believe that it was right to appoint Abu Bakr to be the first Khalifah to lead the Islamic community, Shi'a Muslims argue that the leadership of the community should have stayed within Muhammad's family (ahl al-bayt), and been given to his cousin and son-in law, Ali. This question of succession (imamah) led to a divide within Islam; though both groups stress the need to follow the Six Beliefs of Islam, Shi's Muslims also follow the 'Usal ad-Din, which they regard as the five roots of Islam.

Muslims believe that the Six Beliefs of Islam were revealed by the **ANGEL JIBRIL** (Gabriel) and are recorded in the **HADITH** (sayings from Muhammad, or stories about his life), and also stressed throughout the Qur'an, which says:

> *"Righteous is he who believes in Allah, and the Last Day and the Angels and the Scriptures and the Prophets."*

Qur'an, Surah 2:177

These beliefs or articles of faith are:

- **BELIEF IN ONE GOD** - Allah, who has no equal and is unique; this is known as **TAWHID**
- **BELIEF IN ANGELS (MALAIKAH)** - Spiritual beings who carry out tasks for Allah
- **BELIEF IN THE HOLY BOOKS OF ALLAH** - Primarily the Qur'an, but Allah's will is also revealed through the Sahifah (scrolls), Tawrat (Torah), Zabur (Psalms), and Injil (Gospel of Jesus). The Qur'an fulfils all the other texts
- **BELIEF IN THE PROPHETS OF ALLAH (RISALAH)** - They are chosen by Allah to reveal his will. Muhammad is the Final Prophet, but Muslims believe Allah has chosen 124,000 prophets through whom he has revealed his will
- **BELIEF IN THE DAY OF JUDGEMENT, AND THE AFTERLIFE (AKHIRAH)** - Where all humans will be judged on their deeds, and divided between Jannah (paradise) and Jahannam (hell)
- **BELIEF IN THE WILL OR DECREE (DECISION) OF ALLAH** - Allah has set unchangeable laws in place in the universe (Al-Qadr), but has also given humans free will; Allah knows everything that happens in the universe as he is omniscient

In the 13th Century book the **KITAB AL-IMAN**, by **IBN TAYMIYYAH**, the six beliefs are discussed in detail, and are shown to be what the Qur'an teaches. Taymiyyah's book is part of the Hadith and important within the Sunni tradition of Islam. In the Kitab-al-iman, the story is recorded that Muhammad and a man named Umar were visited by an inquirer (the angel Jibril) who asked Muhammad:

> "Inform me about Iman (faith)."

He (the Holy Prophet) replied:

> "That you affirm your faith in Allah, in His angels, in His Books, in His Apostles, in the Day of Judgment, and you affirm your faith in the Divine Decree about good and evil."

He (the inquirer) said:

> "You have told the truth."

The importance of the Six Beliefs to Muslims today

The six beliefs still form the basis of Islamic belief, and are understood by Muslims to be essential to faith. They are very important principles, and each belief influences what a Muslim does in their life on a daily basis.

Belief in the Oneness of God is essential for Sunni and Shi'a Muslims, and inspires Muslims to believe that Allah is the creator and giver of all things. Without Allah, the universe and humanity would not exist, and this gives reason for Muslims to be thankful to him, and live with gratitude. Muslims recognise that nothing is worthy of worship apart from Allah, and this belief in the Unity or Oneness of Allah helps to bring the Islamic community together. Prayers from the Qur'an remind Muslims that:

> *"He is Allah, there is no God but He. To Him be praise, at the first and the last."*
>
> **28:70**

Belief in angels helps Muslims remain aware of the need to follow Allah's commands. Muslims believe that when they pray, an angel sits on each shoulder, and these angels (kiraman katibeen) record the good and bad deeds of each person. Angels therefore remind Muslims to live a life that is pleasing to Allah and which follows his will. Muslims are also comforted by the presence of angels, though do not pray to them. Surah 9 of the Qur'an reminds believers:

> *"Remember ye implored the assistance of your Lord, and He*

answered you: 'I will assist you with a thousand of the angels, ranks on ranks.'"

Belief in the holy books of Allah helps Muslims to know and follow his will, which is revealed through these scriptures (Kutuballah). Muslims will study and learn from the guidance of the Qur'an and the Hadith in order to know how to live a good life. Teaching on different Muslim scriptures is often given at the mosque. Surah 7:43 reminds Muslims to give:

"Praise to Allah, who has guided us to this. Never could we have found guidance, had it not been for the guidance of Allah."

The prophets of Allah give Muslims examples of how to live, and guidance about what it means to live the sort of life of which Allah approves. Muslims believe that the message of the prophets throughout many centuries has been consistent, which shows that Allah is unchanging and Islam is the true religion. Surah 16:36 states that:

"We sent a messenger to every community, saying, 'Worship God and shun false gods.'"

Belief in the Day of Judgement continually reminds Muslims that their lives will be judged, and that they must remember that all their deeds are seen and noted by Allah. For many Muslims, belief in the afterlife (akhirah) is a positive thing, and gives meaning and purpose to their actions, knowing that their decisions count; Muslims are comforted by the belief that Allah is merciful and just. Muslims are reminded of this each time they attend a funeral. Surah 2:281 reminds Muslims to be:

"Conscious of the Day on which you shall be brought back unto God, whereupon every human being shall be repaid in full."

Belief in the decrees of Allah (Al-Qadr) encourages Muslims to accept the will of Allah as perfect and to trust in his guidance. The belief helps Muslims know that everything happens for a reason. The festival of the Night of Power, Layat al-Qadr, is often a time when Muslims will ask Allah for his blessing on their lives. They are encouraged to repeatedly pray, "I seek the forgiveness of Allah and I repent before Him", so that they recommit to following Allah's will.

THE FIVE ROOTS OF 'USUL AD-DIN

Within the Shi'a tradition of Islam, the five roots or principles of faith are:

- **BELIEF IN THE ONENESS OR UNITY OF GOD (TAWHID)**
  Surah 112 states that:

  "He is Allah, who is one; he neither begets (gives birth) nor is born, nor is there to Him any equivalent."

- **BELIEF IN THE JUSTICE OF GOD, OR DIVINE JUSTICE (AL-ADR)**

- **BELIEF IN PROPHETHOOD (AL-NUBUWWAH)** - From Adam to Muhammad

- **BELIEF IN IMAMS (AL-IMAMAH)**

- **BELIEF IN THE DAY OF RESURRECTION (AL-MA'AD)**

The beliefs in the Oneness of God, Prophethood, and the Day of Resurrection are similar to the beliefs found in the Six Beliefs, as outlined above, and find their roots within the teachings of the Qur'an and the Hadith. There are, however, major differences between Sunni and Shi'a Muslims with regard to the understanding of the status of Imams, and the succession of leadership of the Islamic community (known as imamah) following the death of Muhammad.

Belief in Imams (Al-Imamah)

Following Muhammad's death, many Muslims declared Abu Bakr, Muhammad's father-in-law and trusted advisor, as the next leader and the first Caliph. After Bakr died in 634CE, three other Caliphs were appointed in succession, the last of which was Ali ibn Abi Talib. Sunni Muslims regard these four successors of Muhammad as the "Rightly Guided Caliphs".

However, Shi'a Muslims regard Ali ibn Abi Talib as the true successor of Muhammad, and do not recognise the previous three Caliphs who followed Muhammad. Ali was the cousin and son-in-law of Muhammad and the first male convert to Islam, who Shi'as believe was appointed by Muhammad as his successor. Shi'a Muslims believe that successors to Muhammad should only be from the Prophet's House, or ahl al-bayt.

Differences between Sunni and Shi'a Muslims began over the question of succession to Muhammad and continue today. Shi'a Muslims believe that twelve imams were chosen by Allah, and these were direct descendants of Muhammad. These imams always correctly interpret the Qur'an and the Shariah (Islamic law), as they are inspired by Allah. They are protected by Allah from committing sin, and guard Islam's truth and purity. The Qur'an states that:

> *"God wishes to keep uncleanness away from you, people of the House, and to purify you thoroughly."*
>
> **33:33**

The first eleven imams were killed protecting the faith, and the twelfth imam is a living human being who chooses to meet certain people; this Hidden Imam will be revealed as the Messiah at the end of the world at Makkah, following the second coming of Jesus.

However, Sevener Shi'a Muslims believe that Isma'il ibn Jafar was the seventh and last Imam, and that his son is the eighth and **HIDDEN IMAM** who will return at the end of the world. Twelvers, who make up the majority of Shi'a Muslims, believe that the succession of imams was passed to Isma'il's younger brother and subsequent imams after him down to the Hidden Twelfth Imam.

Whilst both groups accept the five roots of Islam, the major difference between them, apart from the different understanding of the succession of imams, is that the Severners have developed a more mystical path to Allah, whilst the Twelvers have a more literal focus on divine law (Shariah) and the sayings of Muhammad.

In Sunni Islam, the imam leads prayers in the mosque and gives spiritual guidance, and is often the leader of the local Muslim community. An imam can be a member of the congregation rather than an officially appointed person.

The understanding of both the successor to Muhammad, and the status and role of the imam, differs greatly within Shi'a and Sunni Islam.

Belief in Divine Justice (Al-Adl)

The justice of Allah is important to all Muslims, but different understandings exist in Sunni and Shi'a Islam. Shi'a Muslims believe that there are objective moral laws that are right and wrong, and Allah's judgement about human actions will always be right and just.

Using reason, humans can work out what is right and wrong, but Allah alone is perfect and acts with true justice. Shi'a Muslims believe that humans are free, and not pre-destined, to make choices, and do not believe Allah would send a person to hell for something Allah has decided they would do, and over which they had no choice (see exam question at the end of the book).

Concerning the differences between Sunni and Shi'a Muslims on this point, Abbot notes that:

> *"Sunni Muslims question these beliefs, arguing that there is no objective right and wrong, but that everything Allah does is right simply because he does it. They do believe in pre-destination, where Allah determines all human action."*

THE NATURE OF ALLAH

The Qur'an outlines many characteristics of the nature of Allah, and stresses the oneness or uniqueness of him (**TAWHID**).

For example, in **SURAH 16:35**, the instruction is given to:

> *"Serve Allah and shun false gods."*

In **SURAH 163**, Allah is described as:

> *"One. There is no god but He, Most Gracious, Most Merciful."*

As well as references to Allah being One and Unique, he is called, amongst many names (99 in total), compassionate, beneficent, the source of peace, the maker, the provider, the all-forgiving and the generous.

All of these characteristics of Allah belong to the **ONE BEING**.

It is very important to Muslims that Allah is One, because it:

- **RECOGNISES** - Allah has unique status above any other gods (who are false)

- **ACKNOWLEDGES** - There is one creator and sustainer of the world

- **ENABLES** - Muslims to fully focus on one Supreme Being who is uniquely all-knowing and all-powerful. To focus on anything lesser than this in worship is the sin of shirk and completely forbidden

- **SETS ISLAM APART** - From polytheistic religions, and is in distinction to Christian beliefs that God is three persons (Trinity)

Belief in the Oneness of God who created all humanity also helps Muslims regard all people as equal before God, regardless of colour, wealth or race.

Allah is also believed to be both **IMMANENT** - close by - and **TRANSCENDENT** - above and beyond. Surah 50:16 describes how Allah is closer to a man "than his jugular vein." At the same time, Allah is:

> "The Sovereign, the Pure, the Perfection...the Oveseer, the Exalted in Might, the Transcendent. The Superior. Exalted is Allah above whatever they associate with Him."
>
> **Surah 59**

These characteristics are important to Muslims, as though Allah can never be understood, they describe a God who is both involved and active in his creation, but who is not like another being, and who is worthy of adoration and worship as above his creation.

Allah is also described as:

- **OMNIPOTENT** - all powerful

> "Allah is truth, and it is He Who gives life to the dead, and it is He

Who is able to do all things."

22:8

■ BENEFICENT - kind, generous

"Verily, Allah is kind and merciful to the people."

2:143

"Allah is limitless in his great bounty."

3:74

■ MERCIFUL - willing to forgive/show compassion

"Allah is indeed much-forgiving, a dispenser [giver] of grace."

4:96

Alongside this, every surah of the Qur'an starts with a reminder to Muslims that Allah is the Lord of Mercy.

Whilst the above characteristics of Allah demonstrate his love and generosity, as well as his power, it is very important to Muslims that Allah is also just. The kindness and justice of Allah are not opposed, as Allah always acts in kindness even when he punishes, because fair discipline and punishment is necessary to refine a person. For example, although Allah decides certain people go to Hell, many Muslims do not think a person goes there forever, but can go to Paradise once they have been purified. Surah 5:98 notes that Allah is:

"Severe in punishment and forgiving and merciful."

The principle of **DIVINE JUSTICE (ADALAT)** is particularly important in Shi'a Islam, and is one of the **FIVE ROOTS OF 'USU AD-DIN**. Alongside all the other characteristics of Allah, the fact that Allah is just, and will reward and punish fairly and with full knowledge of every person's situation, motives and actions, leads Muslims to reflect carefully upon how they live their lives. This helps to encourage responsibility for actions and also a willingness to seek Allah's forgiveness when believers sin, as Allah is both just and merciful. Muslims believe that if Allah was not merciful and compassionate, no one would survive his judgement.

The Qur'an notes that Allah's justice should be seen in his followers:

> "Allah commands you to return things entrusted (lent) to you to their rightful owners, and if you judge between people, do so with justice. Allah's instructions to you are excellent for He is all-hearing and all-seeing."
>
> 4:58

The qualities that Allah shows in his nature allows Muslims to enter into worship knowing that He is immanent, kind and loving, but also awesome and transcendent in nature. He is to be both trusted and respected greatly at the same time, even when Muslims are going through times of suffering and pain. The characteristics of Allah also act as a motivation for Muslims themselves to try to be beneficent, merciful, loving and just. The Qur'an tells those who believe to be:

> "Upholders of justice, bearing witness for Allah alone, even against yourselves or your parents and relatives."
>
> 4:135

The Qur'an also instructs Muslims to,

> "Uphold justice and do good to others, and give to the relatives' (16:90), and to, 'pardon (people) and overlook (their) faults."
>
> 4:22

RISALAH

Muslims believe that Allah communicates his will to humanity through **PROPHETS**. In Muslim tradition, there are 124,000 prophets, twenty-five of whom are mentioned in the Qur'an. These are people who have been chosen to teach the message of Allah accurately and without fear, so that people can know Allah's will.

This process is called **RISALAH.** Allah communicates his will and guidance to humanity because we are weak and need help knowing how to live. The belief in Risalah is one of the Six Beliefs and also the Five Roots, so is important as it enables Muslims to know Allah's guidance and to understand that he is interested in and cares for them.

Muslims are encouraged to remember the lives of the prophets and the message they gave from Allah:

> *"Muslims, say, 'We believe in Allah and what He has revealed to us and to Abraham, Ishmael, Isaac, and their descendants, and what was revealed to Moses, Jesus, and the Prophets from their Lord.'"*
>
> **2:136**

Muslims do not believe the prophets are equal with Allah, but they are human examples of how to live in submission and obedience to him. The example of how they lived their lives can encourage Muslims to try to act like them. Risalah is important because the prophets bring the guidance of Allah at the right time, and Muslims believe that their message is the same throughout many centuries, showing that Allah is unchanging and Islam is the one true revelation of him. The most prominent prophets in Islam are:

- ### Adam

    Made in Allah's image, Adam is the first human and first representative of Allah on earth (a Khalifa). Adam is made of clay, but Allah also places his spirit in him, with free will and the ability to reason, and he is given the task to care for the earth. Adam is able to answer the questions asked of him by the angels, and all except Satan bow down to him; Satan goes on to try to mislead Adam and all humans.

    Adam is respected by Muslims as he is chosen by Allah, even though he makes a mistake (he does not sin, as prophets cannot sin) by eating from the forbidden tree. Even though Adam and Eve are banished from the beautiful garden in which Allah had placed him, they are shown mercy for this mistake. Muslims understand from the story of Adam not to give in to Satan's temptations but to obey Allah.

- ### Ibrahim (Abraham)

    Described in the Qur'an as a **MAN OF TRUTH**, Ibrahim is respected by Muslims for the example of his great faith in One God and his willingness to stand against the worship of idols.

He was willing to obey Allah's command to leave his home and travel where Allah sent him. He is known as the father of the Arab people, and both his sons become prophets.

Muslims also greatly respect Ibrahim because of his willingness to sacrifice his son Isma'il when asked by Allah; Allah did not require Ibrahim to go through with this sacrifice in the end, but saw and rewarded his faith. The life and pilgrimage of Ibrahim is remembered during the Hajj, and prayers for Allah to bless Ibrahim and his family are said as part of Muslim prayer.

In the Qur'an Ibrahim is called a friend of Allah's - a very great title - and he is greatly respected as the founder of monotheism.

■ Isma'il

Ibrahim's son, Isma'il was willing to be offered as a sacrifice demanded by Allah, for which Allah rewarded him. Muslims believe that when Isma'il's mother Hajar was searching for water in what is now Makkah, Isma'il hit his heel on the ground, which gave rise to a spring. This event is celebrated in the Hajj pilgrimage.

In later life, Isma'il rebuilt the Kaaba (the black stone in Makkah), and, again, he is regarded as an example of faith by Muslims, and someone who completely trusted Allah. Muhammad came from the tribe of Isma'il.

■ Musa (Moses)

Musa was protected by Allah throughout his life, especially when, as a baby, he was placed in a basket on the River Nile, and rescued by a servant in the royal household. The servant was Musa's mother, who ended up caring from him, demonstrating Allah's protection over Musa.

Musa went on to become a great leader of the people of Israel, gaining miraculous victory over Pharaoh and his mighty Egyptian army when escaping through the Red Sea, before seeing Allah's destruction of the Egyptian troops.

After this escape, Allah led Musa and the Israelites, and revealed the Scriptures **(AL-KITAB)** to him, in the form of the **TAWRAT** or **TORAH**, which includes the 10 commandments; these commands are followed by Jews, Christians and Muslims. Allah called Musa an honourable person, and his willingness to persevere, his courage and great trust in Allah, despite setbacks, is regarded as a good example for Muslims to follow.

- ### Dawud (David)

    Dawud is remembered as a great King of Israel who, as a boy, was given victory over Goliath, a giant Philistine enemy, by Allah. Dawud faced opposition throughout his life, but was a great king who led his people in the worship of Allah. Allah revealed Scripture to David - the Psalms of David (Zabur) - which outline reasons why people should praise and worship Allah, and how to pray when distressed or feeling abandoned. Dawud is respected for his wisdom and courage, and both his example, and the Scriptures revealed to him, help Muslims gain strength to follow Allah.

- ### Isa (Jesus)

    Jesus has a place of great respect as a **MOST HONOURED PROPHET** in Islam (though not as the Son of God, as Christians believe). His birth, without a biological father, is recorded as miraculous, and, in his life, he worshipped one God. He saw many miracles of Allah, though Muslims can interpret these symbolically as examples of good overcoming evil, or light beating darkness.

Isa is respected as living in obedience to Allah, but the Qur'an suggests he was saved from the cross rather than killed (as that would be a shameful thing to happen to a prophet of Allah).

Muslims believe that Isa ascended to heaven, and Sunni Muslims believe he will return to earth again. The **INJIL**, or **GOSPEL**, which is included in Islamic Scripture, is the moral teaching revealed to Isa, some of which is preserved in the four Gospels written by his followers.

■ Muhammad

The **FINAL PROPHET OF ISLAM, or SEAL OF THE PROPHETS** (33:41), Muhammad is the final messenger who brings together all previous prophetic revelation in the universal and perfect message of the **QUR'AN**.

He was sent by Allah to bring his truth (61:9), lived a life of obedience to Allah, and, though facing great opposition, formed the community of Islam, and gave the supreme example of what it means to live totally committed to the will of Allah.

At what is remembered as the **LAYLAT AL-QADR (NIGHT OF POWER)**, Allah revealed the first of a series of revelations to Muhammad, which Muhammad was instructed to recite - the word Qur'an means **TO RECITE**. Muslims believe that the words he recited were formed into the Qur'an, and are the direct words of Allah to Muslims today.

The Qur'an says that Muhammad is:

"An excellent model who fears Allah."

33:22

A *"lamp that gives bright light,"*

33:47

MUSLIM HOLY BOOKS - THE KUTUB

Some of the revelations of the prophets mentioned in the previous sections were written down in different books, which are referred to in the Qur'an. This collection of holy books is known as the **KUTUB**, or **KUTUBALLAH**. The holiest revelation from Allah is the Qur'an itself, as this has not been translated or amended. Because of that, it corrects anything that has been lost or distorted in the earlier books.

The Kutub collection

- **The Sahifah** - scrolls of Ibrahim and Musa

    These ancient scrolls are lost but are believed to have contained the revelations received by Ibrahim and Musa. In surah 87, reference is made to the idea that teaching outlined in the Qur'an was in the **BOOKS OF ABRAHAM AND MOSES**, and surah 53 outlines some of the teaching that was in those books, which is in line with the teaching in the Qur'an:

    "He is not acquainted (does not know) what is in the scrolls of Musa and Ibrahim...that no soul shall bear the burden of another, and that there shall be nothing for a man except what he strives (works) for. His effort shall be seen and afterward he will be repaid for it."

- **The Tawrat** - Torah

    Torah is the Hebrew word for Scripture, meaning instruction: The Tawrat was revealed by Allah to Musa (Moses) and given at a specific time when the Israelites were being established as a nation. It is equated to the Jewish Torah or the five books of Moses from the Bible.

    Because it was given at a specific time for a specific group, it is not regarded as universal a text as the Qur'an, but it has teachings in it which are useful for knowing how to live in a way which pleases Allah.

In the Qur'an, it is said that:

"We sent down the Torah, in which was guidance and light. The prophets who submitted to Allah judged by it for the Jews."

The teaching of an **EYE FOR AN EYE**, and a **TOOTH FOR A TOOTH** found in the Torah is quoted in surah 5:45, and, according to surah 7:157, Muhammad is written about in both the Injil (Gospel) revelations to Isa (Jesus), and the Tawrat:

"Those who follow the messenger, the unlettered Prophet, whom they find mentioned in their own (scriptures) - in the law and the gospel."

■ The Zabur - Psalms of Dawud (David)

A collection of songs, prayers, wisdom and poetry from the time of Dawud, and which were used in worship in the Solomon's Temple in Jerusalem. Many were written by Dawud, and they equate to the Psalms in the Old Testament of the Bible. Surah 4:163 makes reference to a line of prophets from Noah forward, and then notes that, "to David we gave the book [of Psalms]." The Zabur is regarded as a holy book in Islam, given by Allah as revelation.

■ The Injil (Gospel) revealed to Isa (Jesus)

This is not quite the same as the four Gospels, Matthew, Mark, Luke and John, which record the life and teaching of Jesus. Muslims regard the Injil as the true Gospel given to Isa by Allah. In surah 5:46, the Qur'an notes that:

"We sent Isa, son of Mary, confirming the Tawrat that had come before him, and we gave him the Injil in which was guidance and light and confirmation of the Tawrat that had come before it."

Muslims believe that the gospel given to Jesus has largely been lost or altered, and there remains part of it recorded in the teaching in the four gospels. However, many Muslims believe the four gospels have been misinterpreted in some places, but that such misinterpretation has now been corrected in the Qur'an. On the other hand, some Muslim scholars don't think that Allah would allow the original Injil to be corrupted.

■ The Qur'an

The final and correct revelation from Allah, given to Muhammad to "recite", and which can be totally trusted. The Qur'an is the holiest and most authoritative source of revelation in Islam, and is the basis of **SHARI'AH LAW**. The true Qur'an should always be read in Arabic, as then there is no need for translation which might alter the meanings of words. Muslims respect the Qur'an as a miracle given by Allah, and study to interpret its meaning, along with the Hadith, for how to live. Muhammad is greatly honoured as someone to whom Allah gave the revelation of the Qur'an. In surah 53, the Qur'an is described as:

"An inspired revelation taught [to Muhammad] by one who is mighty, powerful [angel Gabriel] ... the angel drew near, and revealed to Allah's servant what he was supposed to reveal."

The Qur'an is regarded as the fulfilment of all the other Scriptures that have gone before it, and Muslims believe that, in the previous books, it was said that the Prophet would come (Muhammad) who would receive Allah's final uncorrupted revelation. In surah 10:37, it says,

"This Qur'an is not such as can be produced by other than Allah; on the contrary, it is a confirmation of what went before it, and a fuller explanation of the Book. There is no doubt it is from the Lord of the Worlds."

MUSLIMS regard the books given by Allah as enormously important sources of revelation. The books are used in worship to give guidance and inspiration, whilst the Qur'an is regarded as the full revelation for all humanity. The Qur'an, which brings healing (10:57), says that those who want to be virtuous (good) should follow its teaching (2:177), which Allah has guarded, and will guard from ever being corrupted (15:9). Muhammad followed its teaching, and is therefore seen as an example of a true Muslim. The other texts are also important in giving moral guidance and teaching, providing examples from the prophets of how to submit to Allah's will.

MALAIKAH (ANGELS)

Angels are believed to be spiritual beings, created from light, and are servants of Allah. They do not have free will, but watch over humans; two angels come to the grave to take charge of a person's soul until the Day of Judgement.

Belief in angels is important, and part of the **SIX BELIEFS OF SUNNI ISLAM**. It is not clear what form angels take, as surah 35 says they **HAVE WINGS**, though this is not taken literally by all Muslims, but symbolic of power. Angels are important within Islam because they:

- **BRING MESSAGES FROM ALLAH** - Communicating his guidance to people

- **CARRY OUT TASKS** - Set for them by Allah such as governing the laws of nature and guarding places of worship

- **PROTECT MUSLIMS** - When they pray, and help Muslims when in need

- **COMMUNICATE THE DEEDS OF PEOPLE** - Both good and bad, to Allah

- **STRENGTHEN** - Those who show they have faith in Allah:

"For those who say: 'Our God is Allah'", and then stay firm on it, the angels will descend on them, saying: 'Let nothing fear or grieve you. Rejoice in the good news of paradise that has been promised to you. We are your protectors in this life and the afterlife.'"

41:30

Important angels mentioned in the Qur'an

■ **Jibril** (Gabriel)

Considered an archangel, (the most important of all angels), who was used to reveal Allah's will to several prophets, and, most importantly, recited the Qur'an to Muhammad. Jibril is also regarded as the Holy or Trustworthy Spirit in Islam:

"Jibril brings down the revelation to your heart by Allah's will, a confirmation of what went before, and guidance and glad tidings for those who believe."

2:97-98

Jibril serves Allah's commands - "we angels come down by the command of the Lord", and tells Muslims that Allah is:

"He who is before us, and behind us, ... and the Lord of the heavens and the earth ... without equal."

19:64-5

■ **Izra'il**

Like Jibril, Izra'il is considered an archangel. He is known as the angel of death who separates souls from their bodies and returns them to Allah; he can therefore bring terror to those who do not believe and will be going to hell, but comfort to those going to paradise.

Izra'il is able to recognise the names of those who are blessed and those who are damned, but only Allah knows when a person will die:

"The Angel of Death put in charge of you will take your souls; then you shall be brought back to your Lord."

32:11

Izra'il also descended to earth before the creation of man to bring Allah the materials needed to make Adam.

- **Mika'il** (Michael)

    Mika'il is only mentioned once by name in the Qur'an (see 2:97-8 above). In the Islamic tradition, Mika'il assists Muhammad in fulfilling his spiritual missions, and is believed to provide for humans, both spiritually and physically. He is believed to be the guardian of heaven. Islamic tradition also says that Jibril and Mika'il work the balance of good and bad actions of people on the day of judgement.

- **The kiraman katabin**

    These are angels who are noble scribes (reporters) who sit on the right and left shoulders of every person and take a note of all the good and bad deeds of a person, before presenting these to Allah on the day of judgement.

AL-QADR - PREDESTINATION

Allah is **OMNISCIENT**, which means that he knows everything that happens and will happen. He is in control of all events; surah 13:2 says Allah has:

"Made the sun and the moon submit to his laws, running their course to the term set. He governs all that exists."

Muslims believe that Allah has written all things that will happen in what is called **THE PRESERVED TABLET**, and only he can change what is written there, as surah 13:39 says:

"God annuls (cancels) or confirms whatever He wills from his earlier message. With Him is the Master Copy of the Book."

Muslims believe that Allah cannot be surprised by any action, and nothing can happen unless He wills it. This belief is called **AL-QADR** or **PREDESTINATION**, and it means that Muslims can and should trust Allah in all things, both successes and difficulties, and accept his will. The core of the Islamic faith is to SUBMIT to the will of Allah. For example, Muslims will often say **INSHA ALLAH** to each other when planning an event; insha Allah means "if Allah is willing", and the event would not happen if Allah does not will it to.

The belief in predestination could lead to the danger of fatalism, and believing that there is nothing a person can do that is really their decision, as this has already been decided by Allah. Thus, some Muslims believe that there is no free will (the Jabariyyah school of Islam). However, other Muslims (the Mu'tazilah school of Islam) maintain that humans still have free will and responsibility for their actions, and that predestination does not exist.

Some Muslims raise the problem that, if Allah wills everything, he is responsible for evil and suffering, which is difficult to accept as Allah is beneficent. In addition, some Muslims suggest that it unfair to judge humans on their actions if they have no real control over what they do, and everything has already been planned by Allah.

Differences between different traditions

Most Muslims believe that human beings have free will, but there are different understanding between different traditions:

- **Shi'a Muslims**

    They believe that Allah responds to the prayers of sincere Muslims, and can show mercy to sinners and preserve them from hell. Although Allah knows all things, he can change what he wills, and these changes are already known by him, even though they look like changes to the Muslim who prays. Shi'a Muslims reject absolute predestination, largely due to the belief in **DIVINE JUSTICE** and the idea that it would be unfair for people to be judged for doing things they were always predestined to do.

- **Sunni Muslims**

    They believe that, when a baby receives their soul, 120 days after conception, an angel records whether they will be sent to hell or paradise. The angels go on to record everything a person does in their life and reads those deeds out on the Day of Judgement. Allah's will for us is good, and we can go along with this, or reject it - but Allah knows what we will do.

Abbott writes that:

"Decisions humans make with their free will affect the rewards or punishments from Allah in the afterlife, but Allah already knows what decisions humans will make."

In Sahih Al-Bukhari, one of the Hadiths accepted within the Sunni tradition, it is outlined how, when a man makes a vow to do something, his action will only happen if it agrees with what Allah has decided.

Many Muslims believe that humans can choose to use free will as they decide. Although they cannot change certain things, like the laws of the universe, the genes they have received, or the situation into which they have been born, people can make free decisions on a daily basis.

Muhammad accepted this view of human freedom. He once corrected a friend who said he did not need to tie up his camels because they were in Allah's hands. Muhammad told his friend that they should tie up the camels first and then leave them in Allah's hands.

However, although people are free, Allah knows what each person will choose, and also knows the judgement he will give to people on the **DAY OF JUDGEMENT.**

Belief in qadr is important to Muslims

- **POWERFUL CONTROLLER** - It reminds them of the power and knowledge of Allah, who is in complete control of the universe. Because Allah is in control, nothing happens without a reason
- **PROVIDES OPTIONS** - It does not take away human responsibility for actions; many Muslims believe that humans still have options in front of them, even though Allah knows what option will be taken
- **KIND AND JUST** - It does not take away the goodness of Allah, as he is both kind and just at the same time, and makes correct and fully informed decisions about where people go in the afterlife (akhirah)

However, for other Muslims it is difficult to understand how predestination can be combined with free will, and the idea of life as a test where the result has already been decided.

Without resolving this challenge, many Muslims accept that Allah knows best and what he decides will always be fair and according to his good plan.

AKHIRAH

Muslims believe that this life is a test, and preparation for the afterlife.

At the end of a person's life, the soul is taken by the angel of death, Izra'il, to **BARZAKH**, which is the stage between life and death. Some Muslims believe that, at the **DAY OF JUDGEMENT**, people will be physically resurrected, which is why Muslims do not cremate bodies, and judged by Allah on their actions, which are recorded by angels known as **KIRAMAN KATIBIN**. Other Muslims believe that this is only a spiritual resurrection, and souls will be given new bodies after death.

In all cases, it is believed that Allah knows all the motives and aims behind a person's actions, and will make a fair judgement about whether a person goes to **PARADISE (JANNAH) or HELL (JAHANNAM)**. In surah 17:49-51, non-believers ask:

> *'"What?! When we are reduced to bones and dust, shall we really be raised up again into a new creation?" Tell them, 'Yes, most certainly you shall be brought back to life ....' Then they will ask: 'Who will restore us?' Say: 'The One Who created you the first time.'"*

Before the Day of Judgement, which will be the end of the world, the **MESSIAH (ISA)** will reappear and Islam will be established as the one true religion. The **DAY OF JUDGEMENT** is described as a day when:

> "No soul will have power to do anything for another"

82:19

The judgement itself will be a demonstration of Allah's perfect justice, and those who believe that "there is no true God but Allah, and Muhammad is his Messenger" (the **SHAHADAH** - one of the Five Pillars of Islam) will be admitted to paradise. The decision to send someone to Paradise or Hell is taken by Allah, who holds in balance the good and bad actions, and the faith, of each person.

In surah 18:31, paradise is described as a garden of beauty and peace, where rivers will flow.

People will:

> *"Wear bracelets of gold and green garments of fine silk; they will sit on raised thrones. What an excellent reward and what a beautiful residence."*

Hell is described as:

> *"The fire which is prepared for disbelievers,"*

3:13

over which stand:

> *"Angels, stern and severe, who do not flinch from carrying out Allah's commands."*

66:6

People who are sent there will be in constant pain. These descriptions are not necessarily taken literally by all Muslims, but are given in the Qur'an as a warning to be aware that the actions carried out in life will be rewarded or punished.

Some Muslims argue that, once in Hell, a person is there forever, and, after death, it is not possible to ask for forgiveness:

> *"Surely Allah has laid a curse on the unbelievers and has prepared for them a blazing fire to live there forever, and they shall find no protector or helper."*

33:64-5

Other Muslims believe that only the sin of worshipping something over than Allah (shirk) is unforgivable, and believers (though not unbelievers) will be able to call upon Allah's mercy, as He:

"Forgives all sins. He alone is much-forgiving, a giver of grace."

39:53

The belief in akhirah is essential to Muslims, as it makes sense of this life to have a judgement, which shall be fair and just.

How Akirah affects the way a Muslim lives:

- **EVERY ACTION COUNTS** - It reminds them that every action in this life counts, and gives motivation for doing the right thing

- **PARADISE GUIDE** - It encourages them to follow the guidance in the holy books as the teaching helps them know how to reach paradise, and live well as Allah's representatives on earth

- **PROMOTES CORRECT BEHAVIOUR** - It teaches them to treat others with respect and kindness, and work honestly and with integrity, as Allah rewards such actions

- **REMINDS THEM OF KINDNESS** - It reminds them of the kindness of Allah, as he has prepared paradise for those who follow him, and who have shown faith and carried out good deeds

- **FOCUS ON THE SPIRITUAL** - It teaches Muslims to concentrate on spiritual things, and not be so focused on building up material riches in this life, which should be shared with the poor, and that are of no use in the afterlife

Similarities of belief in Akhirah with Christian beliefs in the after life

There are many similarities between Muslim and Christian believes in the afterlife but also many differences.

- **Judgement**

    Muslims believe that the soul shall be taken to **BARZARKH** between a person dying and a person being judged

    Christians believe that the soul leaves the body at the time of death

and awaits the resurrection of the body on the **DAY OF JUDGEMENT**

■ Resurrection

Some Muslims believe in a physical resurrection, whilst others believe in a spiritual resurrection only.

Some Christians believe in a physical resurrection, whilst others believe in a spiritual resurrection only.

■ Omniscience

Muslims believe that Allah knows everything and will make a perfect judgement on a person's life.

Christians believe that God knows everything and will make a perfect judgement on a person's life.

Differences of belief in Akhirah with Christian beliefs in the afterlife.

■ Judgement

Muslims believe that the actions of a person's life will be judged and that will be the basis upon which a person will go to paradise or hell.

Christians believe that Jesus has paid for the sins of everyone who asks to be forgiven, and that a person's deeds, however good, will never be enough to please God, but trust in Jesus' death will.

■ Who is saved

Muslims believe that Allah divides people between paradise and hell.

Some Christians believe in hell, whilst others believe that God will save everyone.

KEYWORDS

- **APOSTASY** - Leaving a religion

- **BLASPHEMY** - Offending religious beliefs, eg disrespecting a prophet

- **BLOOD MONEY** - Money paid by the murderer to the victim's relatives

- **CAPITAL PUNISHMENT** - The death penalty; punishment by execution

- **CRIME** - An action, or failure to carry out an action, that breaks the law and is punishable by law

- **DETERRENCE** - The use of punishment to deter or discourage other people from offending

- **FAIR TRIAL** - An independent trial without prejudice, and which respects all participants right to a fair hearing under law

- **FITRAH** - Human nature, with which we are born

- **FORGIVENESS** - To grant pardon for an offence or sin

- **HUMAN RIGHTS** - Rights to which all people are entitled

- **JUSTICE** - The quality of being just, impartial or fair

- **MADINAH CHARTER** - A document by Muhammad outlining laws for how to carry out justice

- **PROTECTION** - Punishing a criminal in such a way that they cannot harm other people or society, eg by keeping them in prison

- **PUNISHMENT** - A penalty given to a person because they have broken the law

- **QADI** - A judge in Muslim law

- **QISAS** - Retaliation or revenge fitting the crime

- **PROTECTION** - Keeping safe from harm

- **REFORMATION** - Punishment which aims to change someone's behaviour for the better

- **RESTORATION** - Restoring someone who has done wrong

- **RESTORATIVE JUSTICE** - A form of justice that focuses on restoring peace by reconciling criminals and victims and society in order to rehabilitate offenders

- **RETRIBUTION** - Punishment which is carried out for the purposes of repayment or revenge for the wrong act committed

- **SHARI'AH** - Islamic law based on the teaching of the Qur'an, Sunnah and Hadith, and scholarly understanding of those documents

- **SITUATION ETHICS** - A method of trying to do the most loving thing in each situation

- **TORTURE** - The action of inflicting severe pain; in this section, inflicting pain as a punishment or to force a person to say or do something

- **TRIAL BY JURY** - Where a case is heard before a jury under the guidance of a judge

- **UNITED NATIONS** - International organisation of member states formed to promote peace and justice, and the respect of human rights

- **UTILITARIANISM** - Ethical theory in which the right thing to do is that which maximises happiness and minimises pain

JUSTICE

Justice concerns the right and fair treatment of people according to law, ensuring that society is a place of respect and safety for all people. It upholds respect for the law and enables individuals to live and work without fear in society. Justice also allows for the innocent to be protected and the guilty punished under law, both having access to a fair and unbiased treatment in the judicial system.

Justice is important to Muslims as, when it is upheld, it shows respect for Allah, whose name is Just. Allah's nature is to be just, and Muslims want to reflect this in the way that they live and organise society:

> *"Allah has set up the balance of justice in order that you should not transgress [break the law]."*
>
> **Surah 55:7**

If Muslims work for justice, they will receive good judgement when Allah judges all people. By giving **ZAKAH** and showing kindness to the vulnerable, Muslims try to ensure all people have access to fairness and justice in life. Muslims do not charge interest on loans in order to avoid taking advantage of the poor, and getting rich through exploitation would not be a just action.

Justice ensures that all people are treated without bias and with fairness.:

> *"Stand firm for justice and bear true witness for the sake of Allah, even though it be against yourselves, your parents or your relatives. It does not matter whether the party is rich or poor - Allah is well-wisher of both. So let not your selfish desires swerve you from justice. If you distort your testimony or decline to give it, then you should remember that Allah is fully aware of your actions."*

Justice ensures that people are not oppressed, as the hadith of Riyad al-Salihin instructs. All people at different levels of society should be protected by justice and equal treatment under law.

Muslims argue that justice is very important for the victims of maltreatment

If someone has been wronged, it is important to Muslims to protect them and find a just outcome. If someone has wronged another person, it is important that the victim's claim for justice is heard first before the perpetrator can ask for forgiveness. This upholds respect for the law and the process of justice being applied, through appropriate punishment if that is the outcome. It is also important in Islam that no one is punished who is actually innocent.

Muslims argue that it is also important to view justice as wider than situations that are covered by law or the legal system. People who are victims include those born in poverty, who struggle for clean water and to provide for their children, and to whom basic human rights such as education are not available. Muslims work to create and deliver justice in such situations through organisations such as Islamic Aid.

Non-religious attitudes towards justice and why it is important

Although not motivated by the idea of bringing Allah's justice on earth, or reflecting his nature, many people who take a **HUMANIST** or **ATHEIST** approach to issues of injustice work to help bring justice for victims. Because a central aim of humanism is for humanity to flourish, it is important that where that is not happening, people act to restore dignity, hope and justice.

The British Humanist Association notes that:

> "Man should show respect to man, irrespective of class, race or creed. [This is] fundamental to the humanist attitude to life. Among the fundamental moral principles, he would count those of freedom, justice, tolerance and happiness."

MUSLIMS WOULD AGREE with atheists and humanists in having the same aim of bringing about justice for victims and protecting and supporting those who are likely to face injustice.

Whilst Muslims would uphold Muhammad as the most excellent model of how to live a just life, there are many areas of overlap between Muslims and non-religious groups in aiming for universal justice, where all people are given fair trial under law, and everyone has the chance to have access to a good life.

An area of disagreement between Muslim and non-religious attitudes would be that Muslims believe ultimate justice belongs to Allah, as depending on human reason is not enough, and examples of the lack of justice in human societies and in law have been seen throughout history. Without the guidance of the Qur'an and Islamic teaching, Muslims believe that law will not reflect ultimate principles of what is right and just, true and fair.

CRIME

A crime is something that someone does, like theft, or fails to do, like not declaring income to avoid tax, that breaks a law. The person who breaks the law is punishable by the justice system.

The causes of crime are complex

Many factors contribute to why a crime takes place. These include:

- **MATERIALISM** - The need or want for money or possessions
- **ADDICTION** - The need to feed an addiction
- **EMOTIONAL** - Envy, anger or revenge
- **OPPORTUNITY** - Family upbringing and poor educational performance that can lead to a lack of opportunity to get good employment
- **PEER PRESSURE** - And/or negative stereotyping and discrimination against a social group, leading to isolation and possibly crime
- **GREED**
- **POVERTY**

■ **MENTAL ILLNESS**

The nature of crime

This is also complex and ranges from theft and robbery, to harm to a person, damage to property, to tax evasion and fraud. Crime can be committed by people of a range of backgrounds, with deliberation or spontaneously, against strangers or those known to the person, or a group or corporation, and over differing lengths of time.

In Shari'a Law there are strict penalties laid down for the breaking of law, but also limitations on those penalties, so that they are not overly harsh. There are three types of crime in Islamic law:

- **HUDUD** - Meaning limit or boundary. These are crimes against Allah and the boundaries he has established, and include things such as unlawful sexual intercourse. Such crimes cannot be pardoned by the state or victim

- **QISAS** - Crimes against man; in these cases the victim or the victim's family can choose the preferred penalty

- **TA'ZIR** - Refers to punishment that is decided by an Islamic judge - a **QADI** - as the punishment is not laid down in the Qur'an or Sunnah or Hadith

Muslim teaching about crime

Instruction is given to Muslims regarding crime:

> "Allah commands doing justice, doing good to others, and giving to near relatives, and He forbids indecency, wickedness and rebellion: He admonishes [instructs] you so that you may take notice. Be true to your bond with Allah whenever you bind yourselves by a pledge, and do not break oaths after having confirmed them and having called upon Allah to be your witness. Allah knows all that you do."
>
> **Surah 16:90-92**

It goes on to instruct Muslims not to deceive each other, as Allah will make it clear on Judgement Day what the deception was.

From this teaching Muslims know that:

- **ALLAH IS A JUST Allah** - He expects believers to also be just and do good to others

- **BE RESPECTFUL** - Allah expects Muslims to live in a way that is decent and respectful, both to themselves and others, not being wicked or rebelling

- **NO BAD BEHAVIOUR** - Allah has made it clear that his teachings are there to guide people so that people cannot make excuses about not knowing how to behave

- **KEEP PROMISES** - Allah expects a person's promises to Him and to others to be kept

- **DO NOT SIN** - Allah knows all that people do, so any crime that is not detected is still known by him and will be taken into account at the Day of Judgement

Things that distract Muslims from following Allah

Muslims sometimes commit crimes or go against Allah's laws because they are distracted. The Qur'an in surah 4:50 instructs Muslims to continue to obey Allah. In surah 5:93-4 Muslims are told that Satan uses intoxicants (such as **DRUGS** and **ALCOHOL**) to keep people away from Allah and his path. Muhammad said that anything that clouds the mind or changes a person's sensible reasoning is forbidden. **SMOKING** is not mentioned in the Qur'an or by Muhammad, but is regarded as **MAKRUH** - not haram, but disliked.

Muslims might suggest that the teaching against substances such as alcohol once again shows how perfect the Qur'an is in guiding people, as many crimes are committed which involve alcohol consumption. The Crime Survey of England and Wales in 2014/15 recorded that there were 592,000 violent incident where the victim believed the offender/s to be under the influence of alcohol, accounting for 47% of violent offences committed that year.

In surah 5:90-91 **GAMBLING** is mentioned as another thing that Satan will use to distract believers from following Allah. Gambling can take over a person's rational abilities and lead to much hardship for a family.

Muslim action to help end crime

■ Muslim Hands

Muslim Hands is an organisation which attempts to:

"Be good to the neighbour who is your relative and to the neighbour is who not a relative"

4:36

It does this by:

- ■ **CRIME AVOIDANCE** - Working to provide education and opportunities in Muslim communities in order to help people avoid committing crimes. It states that 46% of people who identify as Muslim in the UK live in the most deprived areas, and is therefore trying to bring justice into those areas in practical ways to build **BETTER OUTCOMES**

- ■ **IMPROVE EDUCATION** - Working with families and in schools to raise child literacy, providing help to prisoners in their rehabilitation once released from prison, putting into place long term strategies to reduce poverty, empowering women with the skills needed to cope well with life in the UK, and working with local community groups to boost the confidence of young Muslims in order to help them achieve employment and social skills

■ The Muslim Chaplains Association

The MCA provides spiritual and pastoral support to Muslim prisoners, and, upon release, offers a mentoring service between a newly released prisoner and a former prisoner who has settled back into the community; in order to help reduce reoffending. The MCA works in the community to encourage Muslims to care for those released from prison to reduce the chance of them committing further crime.

■ Mosaic

Mosaic offers a programme for prisoners and former prisoners aged between 18 and 30 which provides:

"Focused support and mentoring opportunities around the vulnerable period of transition from custody back into the community."

Working to find housing and employment with those just released and prisoners coming to the end of their sentences reduces the chance of reoffending. Trained mentors offer both practical and emotional support to enable the prisoner to be rehabilitated into society.

These actions are practical ways in which Muslims can fulfil two of the Ten Obligatory Acts to encourage good actions (**AMR BIL MA'ROOF**) and discourage bad actions (**NAHI ANIL MUNKAR**).

GOOD, EVIL AND SUFFERING

The Qur'an makes it clear that Allah is the creator of all things, and that human beings were created by him with an innate sense of right and wrong. The nature, o**r FITRAH,** with which humans are born is pure:

"Stand firm in your devotion to the upright faith - the nature made by Allah, the one on which mankind is created."

30:30

This means that humans, as created by Allah, are naturally inclined to do good by instinct, but often do not submit their way to Allah and choose evil instead. The Hadith of Saheeh notes that:

"I created My servants in the right religion, but the devils made them go astray."

Unlike in some Christian thought, for Muslims evil is not the absence of good, but a real choice of following the opposite of what is intended for people, and not staying true to the nature given to them by Allah.

Because humans have free will, they are allowed to choose evil, or follow the influence of Satan or others, and use what Allah has allowed for bad purposes. Even though people are badly influenced - sometimes by parents - they still have a duty to follow the right way:

> *"We advise man to be good to his parents, but if they try to make you do in My name what you know to be false, do not obey them."*
>
> **29:8**

Apart from things such as gambling and alcohol, nothing in the world is bad or good by itself, eg, a car is good for transport but can be used to cause harm, but there will be consequences for how people have freely responded to the choices in front of them:

> *"It is quite possible that something which you don't like is good for you and that something which you love is bad for you. Allah knows, and you do not."*
>
> **2:216**

If a person continues to follow their own way, they may end up in a state of unbelief, or **KUFR**. This can result in a craving for things that Allah has said is not good for people, and a misuse of the gifts Allah has given. In this life, there are chances to repent of such deeds, before Judgement Day calls all human actions to account. In this way evil is a test for humans to overcome, and is the opposite of good and Allah's will. But evil is also temporary as everything in this world is only present for a short time, as part of the test for humans; they need to pass this test in order to have permanent and eternal life in paradise after death, where there is no evil.

Reward for living a good life

The reward of a paradise in the afterlife is described in several places in the Qur'an as a garden of delights, (eg surah 76's description of fruit, beautiful garments, silver plates and goblets) though many take this as metaphorical language trying to describe a state of bliss that is impossible to capture in human language. Surahs 32 and 76 both say that when believers look there (paradise) they will see a delight that cannot be imagined.

Divergent Muslim teaching about suffering

Muslims agree that Allah is omnipotent and omniscient, and alone knows the reason why there is suffering in the world. It is sometimes difficult for humans to grasp why pain and evil exist, but Muslims are encouraged to submit to the will of Allah, and to remember that this life is only short before great reward comes in the afterlife for those who faithfully follow Allah's will.

Muslims believe that suffering is a test - Man is insignificant, and created:

> *"From a drop of mingled fluid to put him to the test,"*

and should not be surprised when faced with difficulties

Surah 76:1

> *"Do you think that you will enter paradise without any trials?"*

2:214

This test has a real result at the end, either of reward as described above, or great suffering in hell, described in as a:

> *"Blazing fire for the unbelievers."*

Surah 76

Muslims believe that suffering can result from Satan causing people to go astray from Allah's will, which is always a bad choice:

> *"O you who believe, do not follow the steps of Satan. Anyone who follows the steps of Satan should know that he advocates evil and vice."*

24: 21

This does not excuse humans, however, as the Qur'an notes that:

> *"Anything good that happens to you is from Allah, anything bad is from your own soul"*

4:79

As part of this, ignoring the warnings and teachings of the prophets and going one's own way can only lead to disaster; surah 64 warns that rejecting the message of the prophets will lead to a painful torment.

The Muslim explanation for the nature of good and evil actions and the causes of suffering is very different to the responses of non-religious people, including people who are **HUMANISTS** or **ATHEISTS**.

Both **HUMANISM** and **ATHEISM** teach that:

- **THERE IS NO ALLAH WHO GAVE HUMANS FREE WILL** - Humans have freedom, but it is not given by Allah as part of a test. Humanists acknowledge that people can be extraordinarily cruel and unjust but choices people make are not part of a test as Muslims believe. Sometimes suffering happens as a result of bad luck rather than as part of a pre-ordained plan or obstacle to overcome.

- **THERE IS NO REWARD OR PUNISHMENT** - In an afterlife for good or bad actions, as there is no afterlife or Deity to carry out that judgement. People, using their reason correctly, can be good without Allah's help, or without the hope of reward or fear of punishment for not acting rightly.

- **NO EVIL** - Many humanists and atheists are reluctant to use the term "evil", as it is associated with "actions against Allah". If referring to bad actions, humanism would suggest these are depraved or shameful rather than evil

- **PEOPLE ARE RESPONSIBLE** - In agreement with Islam, atheists and humanists agree that people are entirely responsible for their voluntary actions, and should work towards relieving suffering and pain wherever they can

- **EVERYONE HAS A CONSCIENCE** - Islam, atheism and humanism would agree that everyone has a conscience and some knowledge of what it means to **DO THE RIGHT THING**. They would disagree that the cause and source of that conscience is part of a Allah-given nature

In response to atheist and humanist approaches, Muslims teach that there is a need for an ultimate explanation about the nature of good and evil, and why people do good and bad deeds; there is a need for a Allah who sees all intentions behind actions, which no one else sees.

Evil and suffering only make sense if our response to them is judged, and either punished or rewarded, as this gives meaning and purpose to life; otherwise we might as well live as we wish without thought of what impact our actions have on others. Suffering gives Muslims a chance to show

Allah's mercy and kindness to others in times of need, by working to relieve suffering and pain.

PUNISHMENT

Punishment is intended to uphold justice in society

Islam teaches that, to help maintain an ordered and peaceful society, punishment for the breaking of laws should be in place. The nature of the punishment should respect the rights of the victim, and uphold the dignity of the criminal, even when the law has been broken.

Muslim teaching

"Retaliation is prescribed for you in the case of murder; a free man for a free man, a slave for a slave and a female for a female. But if anyone is pardoned by his aggrieved brother, then blood money [a ransom for manslaughter] should be decided according to the common law and payment should be made with gratitude. This is a concession and a mercy from your Lord. Now, whoever exceeds the limits after this, shall have a painful punishment."

Surah 2:178

This teaching promotes the idea of **QISAS** and is encouraged for Muslims.

Justice is delivered by holding the criminal to account and giving a just sentence to them in retribution for what they have done. The punishment fits the crime (a free man for a free man etc), so that in the case of murder, capital punishment is allowed.

However, the family of the person who has had the crime committed against them can decide upon the most fitting form of punishment, which could be the demand for **BLOOD MONEY** from the criminal. This could combine both mercy and justice, two attributes of the nature of Allah, and can happen between families within the Ummah. Blood money has to be paid promptly and with an indication that the person who committed the crime has fully repented of what they have done.

This type of system could link to **SITUATION ETHICS** as it takes each case on its merits and decides what the appropriate punishment would be in that situation. It allows for love to be demonstrated in the form of a just punishment, such as blood money, which attempts to restore the criminal after they have paid their dues.

Surah 5:44-48

Whilst most Muslims believe that the above teaching from surah 2 is only for Muslims, the teaching in surah 5 refers to all people who follow the one true Allah - the **KITAB** or people of the book, Jews, Christians and Muslims. It states that when the light of the Torah was given it prescribed as punishment:

"A life for a life, an eye for an eye ... and for a wound an equal retaliation. If anyone remits the retaliation through charity it will be an act of atonement for him. Those who do not judge by the law which Allah has revealed are the wrongdoers."

Just as the above was a guide to Jews, Christians were given guidance in the Gospel, but the Qur'an fulfils both of those Scriptures, and instructs people of the book that the Qur'an:

"Confirms whatever has remained intact in the scriptures which came before it, and also to safeguard it. Therefore, judge between people according to Allah's revelations and do not yield to their vain desires diverging from the truth which has come to you. We have ordained a law and a Way of life for each of you."

Allah has ordained that there are different races and groups in society, but has laid down law and a system of justice, and whoever follows this has successfully followed his will.

Why punishment is needed in society

- **TO DEMONSTRATE ALLAH'S JUSTICE ON EARTH** - To show that people are responsible for their actions. Crime goes against the desire of Muslims to create a society of order and peace, and punishment needs to be in place to bring that about

- **THE RULE OF LAW IS TO BE UPHELD** - Punishment should be carried out, because without sufficient deterrent people might feel free to commit crime

- **SOCIETY SHOULD BE A SAFE AND FAIR PLACE** - Punishment of criminals can help make society both safer, through the removal of a criminal from society, either through death or imprisonment, and fairer through just sanctions

- **APPROPRIATE PUNISHMENT MAY HELP** - The criminal might realise what they have done is wrong, and enable them to be reformed and rehabilitated into society

THE AIMS OF PUNISHMENT

Laws aim to put justice into practice in a society

When laws are broken, punishment takes place, and different types of punishment have different aims:

- **PROTECTION** - This aims to protect society from criminals who could be a danger to people, and to themselves, if allowed to stay in society

- **RETRIBUTION** - This aims to make criminals pay for what they have done wrong. It is carried out to deliver justice to the victim of crime if the criminal is given a fitting sentence which 'pays' for their offence, as allowed under QISAS

- **DETERRENCE** - This aims to make the punishment of such a nature that people will be put off, or deterred, from committing a crime

- **REFORMATION** - This aims to provide opportunities for the criminal to reflect upon their actions, and to reform, so that they can be restored or rehabilitated into society, and not commit further crime

There are **DIFFERENT VIEWS** among Muslims about the aims of punishment, and support for all 4 different types.

The aim of punishment in Islam is to both uphold law and create a just society, rather than carry out harsh sentences that severely damage an individual person. At times, this will mean that the punishment removes a criminal from society - either by capital punishment or a prison sentence - in order to give **PROTECTION** to its citizens.

Any seemingly severe punishment, such as the cutting off of hands from thieves (permitted in surah 5:38) is meant to lead to **REFORM**, and must only be carried out under strict conditions. In practice, it is carried out in very specific circumstances where Shari'ah law is strictly applied in Iran and Saudi Arabia. Even then, a person can be forgiven by Allah if they repent (surah 5:39).

However, many Muslims believe that once a criminal has committed a crime against Allah (huddu) they should be publicly shamed and punished in such a way that **RETRIBUTION** is ensured:

> "The reward for an injury is an equal injury back"

Surah 42:40

It is not for a human court of law to challenge such teaching. This punishment is also able to **DETER** others from committing crime, and can lead to justice and the law being restored and respected in society:

> "Allah orders justice and good conduct and giving to relatives and forbids immorality and bad conduct and oppression. He admonishes you that perhaps you will be reminded."

16:90

Other Muslims stress the mercy of Allah, and that forgiveness is possible if a person is truly sorry for their sin:

> "If a person forgives instead, and is reconciled, that will earn reward from Allah."

16:90

> "If an enemy starts leaning towards peace, then you also start leaning towards peace."

8:61

In this view, Muslims recognise that everyone needs forgiveness from Allah and a second chance, which emphasises Allah's mercy.

The Qur'an emphasises both the **JUSTICE** and **MERCY** of Allah. Surah 4:26-32 states that the laws have been clearly laid down, but that Allah wishes to show mercy as he recognises that humans are weak. It goes on to say:

> "Do not consume one another's wealth through unlawful means; instead, do business with mutual consent; do not kill each other (or yourself) by adopting unlawful means ... anyone who commits such acts of aggression and injustice will soon be thrown into hellfire."

How Muslims are guided by this teaching

- **UPHOLD AND RESPECT THE LAW** - Muslims are instructed to abide by the law

- **TREAT EACH OTHER WITH RESPECT** - And live at peace with others

- **RESPECT LIFE** - This could refer to one's own life, as well as that of others, and could also refer to a spiritual death rather than a physical death

- **BE PUNISHED** - Realise that there is real punishment from Allah if one acts with injustice

- **TAKE CARE NOT TO COMMIT SINS WHICH ARE GREAT** - Smaller sins can be forgiven if a person tries to avoid great sins

- **NOT TO BE ENVIOUS OF OTHERS** - As that can lead to sin and crime

- **BE FAIRLY REWARDED** - Be confident that Allah, because of his grace and mercy, and his knowledge of all things, will reward people fairly

The remaining verses of the passage in Surah 4 guides Muslims further:

"If you avoid the great things which are forbidden, We will remit from you your evil deeds and make you enter at a noble gate. Do not envy that Allah has given some of you more than the others. Men will be rewarded according to their deeds and women will be rewarded according to theirs. Ask Allah for His grace. Surely Allah has perfect knowledge of everything."

Surah 4:26-32

FORGIVENESS

Forgiveness is to grant pardon for an offence or sin or wrong-doing, and to stop blaming someone for the thing they have done wrong

As every surah of the Qur'an begins by naming Allah as the Lord of mercy, Muslims know that Allah's mercy and forgiveness is possible, but not to be taken lightly. Forgiveness does not excuse the wrongful act or sin, or take away a punishment, but means that the penalty for that sin deals with it properly, and there is no need for continual retribution, once that sin has been forgiven.

This is shown in surah 64:9, where at the Day of Judgement:

"Those who believe in Allah and do good deeds, he will remove from them their sins and admit them to gardens beneath which rivers flow, to live therein forever, and that will be the supreme achievement."

One of the good deeds that Muslims can do is to **FORGIVE OTHERS**, which reflects the character of Allah, who is sometimes called **THE FORGIVING ONE.** Muhammad chose to forgive when he commanded that no retribution should be taken by his followers against those who had persecuted them in Makkah; this acts as an example for Muslims in knowing how to restore justice. Muhammad also taught that:

"If you show mercy to those on earth He who is in heaven will

show mercy to you."

Furthermore in the Hadith of Hasan al-Basri, it is noted that:

"The best attribute a believer can have is forgiveness."

FORGIVENESS IS THE FOUNDATION OF RESTORATIVE JUSTICE, in which the offender and the victim work through a process which enables the victim to receive justice, whilst the offender:

- **IS ASKED TO REPENT** - And realise the seriousness of their offence
- **RECEIVES FORGIVENESS**
- **IS RECONCILED** - With those they have offended
- **IS RESTORED TO SOCIETY**

It is important to the offender that this process takes place in order for them to be fully restored into the community, and for their crime not to be continually held against them, which would stop them from moving on from the past. Similarly, restorative justice can bring healing to the victim and help them build their lives again.

The Centre for Restorative Justice and Peacemaking (CRJP) describes restorative justice as the attempt to:

"Respond to crime and violence by using dialogue, [working towards] repair of harm, and peace-building [in order to] heal victims, and bolster social harmony."

Restorative justice relies on repentance, forgiveness and reconciliation, all of which reflect the mercy of Allah. The qisas form of justice allows for the victim of the crime to show mercy whilst asking for a recompense from the offender. The CRJP notes that:

"The Qur'an presents a range of retaliatory/punitive compensatory and reconciliatory measures from which to choose, and often suggests relying on restorative principles."

For example, surah 5:8 says that people are not to be overtaken with hatred when wronged:

"You who believe! Stand out firmly for Allah, as witnesses to fair dealing, and let not the hatred of others to you make you swerve to wrong and depart from justice. Be just; that is next to piety [goodness, purity]."

Teaching is given to believers regarding justice:

"Believers, even among your spouses and the children [you have] there are enemies; be wary of them but if you see over [overlook] their offences, forgive them, pardon them, and Allah is all-forgiving, the merciful."

Surah 64:14

Restorative justice is necessary to rebuild a society and allow for peaceful relationships to be restored. It is a form of justice supported by many Muslims and modelled by Muhammad in the **MADINAH CHARTER**. Muhammad outlined that this type of justice, in which the victim and the offender are reconciled, most reflects Allah's wish for a peaceful and just society, though this is not easy for either party. However, this type of justice helps to restore the criminal whilst powerfully confronting them with the impact their crime had on the victim, realising that crime has a very real human cost.

A modern day example of restorative justice in action was when the US Attorney General asked the Muslim community what punishment they thought would be suitable for a Texan man who made a bomb threat against the Islamic centre in Murfreesboro, Tennessee, in 2011. The imam replied that he would like the man to join with the Islamic community for 50 hours so that he would interact with Muslims and there would be opportunity for relationships to be built and reconciliation to be put into practice.

THE TREATMENT OF CRIMINALS

One of the 99 names of Allah is **THE JUST** from the Arabic **AL-ADL**. Brown points out that this literally means "putting things in their correct place", and that applies to how Muslims view the justice system: the victims should be given due regard and treated with justice, but, at the same time, the human rights of the criminal should be respected. Both the Qur'an and the way in which Muhammad treated people show how to treat all people with dignity, and many of the same rights that were later put forward in the **UNITED NATIONS DECLARATION OF HUMAN RIGHTS** in 1948 were already part of Muslim belief and practice.

The aim of Muslims is to establish the ways of Allah on earth, and to bring about peace and justice in society:

> "O you who believe! Enter absolutely into peace."
>
> Surah 2:208

Surah 48 encourages Muslims to:

> "Compete with each other in doing good."

These teachings, and historical examples of how Muhammad behaved, mean that Muslims should treat criminals humanely, even though they have:

> "Made mischief on the land, [and have not] mended their ways"
>
> Surah 26:152

Muslims also realise that they themselves are in need of Allah's mercy and kindness, and are told:

> "None of you believes (in truth) unless he loves his brother that which he loves from himself."

Hadith Sahih Muslim 1:17

So it is important that Muslims treat criminals in a way that they themselves would wish to be treated.

SURAH 76 outlines clear expectations for how a criminal should be treated, and the humane treatment outlined was against cultural expectations at the time. The surah starts off by reminding Muslims that Allah has guided people whether or not they have followed that guidance, and some haven't.

Some people, because of their disobedience, will receive an afterlife which is harsh – with:

> "Chains and shackles and a blaze."

As for those who follow Allah, they are ones who give:

> "Food in spite of love for it to the needy, the orphan and the captive."

Their motivation for doing this is not for reward or gratitude, but "for the countenance of Allah."

It is clear that Muslims are not to deprive a criminal of their basic rights, which was something that was happening in the time of Muhammad when soldiers were captured. Allah is looking for justice to be followed, and people will be judged on how they have carried it out:

> "Stand firm for Allah, witnesses in justice, and do not let the hatred of a people prevent you from being just. Be just; it is near to righteousness; and fear Allah; Allah knows what you do."

Surah 5:8

Different Muslim attitudes towards the treatment of criminals

Although the guidance and teaching above is respected by Muslims, there are different beliefs about how criminals should be treated.

Some argue that **TORTURE** is permitted by surahs such as 5:33 (amputation) and 8:12:

> "Remember thy Lord inspired the angels (with the message): 'I am with you: give firmness to the Believers: I will instil terror into the hearts of the Unbelievers: smite above their necks and smite all their fingertips off them.'"

Surah 24:2 outlines flogging with one hundred stripes for both people involved in cases of adultery.

But the majority of Muslims do not support torture or the cruelty of groups such as IS. Teaching given in Illinois by the Council for Social Justice states that:

> "Torture in Islam is considered a major violation to the fundamental rights of someone or of some living being. It occurs when undue pain or suffering is inflicted upon a living creature; a creation of Allah Almighty. Muslims know that every act of aggression done to others, no matter how small or how large, will be questioned on the Day of Judgment. It is because of this thorough questioning in the court of justice of Allah Almighty on this day that a Muslim should avoid harm and injury to others lest he brings himself to total ruin."

As a result of this approach, many Muslims would reject the ideas held within **SITUATION ETHICS**, that torture could be used if it benefited the greater good, which would be a loving thing to do, as that would go against the rights of the individual criminal.

Most Muslims support justice for the criminal through the use of a **FAIR TRIAL** and **TRIAL BY JURY**. Watton and Stone note that, where western practices have been adopted in Islamic courts, a jury is used, but Shari'ah law does not require one:

> "Crimes against Allah's law (including drinking alcohol, lending

with interest, committing adultery) are prosecuted by the state as **HADD** *crimes, and all other criminal matters are treated as disputes between individuals, with an Islamic judge deciding the outcome based on Shari'ah."*

However, Ahmedi notes that processes such as trials in front of a jury were introduced by Islam before any other legal system in England.

The picture is mixed because there are different practices in different countries around the world, where different legal systems are in place. But, in Islam, teaching about the treatment of criminals should ensure the respect of their basic human rights.

THE DEATH PENALTY

Capital punishment, or the death penalty, was permanently abolished in the UK in 1970

However, it is still legal in over 70 countries, including 37 of 50 US states. Most Muslims accept the death penalty for certain crimes, but, there is a minority Muslim view against the use of the death penalty, with argument against suggesting that the much better solution is the giving of **BLOOD MONEY** to the victim's family.

Muslim attitudes for the death penalty

- **Capital punishment is set down by Allah**

    In the Qur'an:

    "Take not life, which Allah has made sacred, except by way of justice and law."

    Surah 6:51

- **In Shari'ah law, the collective implementation of the Qur'an and the Hadith, scholars support the death penalty for:**

- **INTENTIONAL MURDER**

- **SPREADING MISCHIEF IN THE LAND** - Which can include treason or apostasy (leaving the faith), terrorism, rape, adultery, homosexual activity and, in some countries, blasphemy

- **APOSTASY** - In the case of apostasy:

"They wish that you reject Faith, as they have rejected (Faith), and thus that you all become equal (like one another). So take not Auliya' (protectors or friends) from them, till they emigrate in the Way of Allah (to Muhammad). But if they turn back (from Islam), take (hold) of them and kill them wherever you find them, and take neither Auliya' (protectors or friends) nor helpers from them."

Surah 4:65

■ Muhammad agreed with capital punishment

The Prophet said: "It is not permissible to take the life of a Muslim except in one of the three cases: the married adulterer, a life for a life (if the person is Muslim), and the deserter of Islam."

Hadith, Muslim 16:452

These are three very important sources of authority for Muslims, and many believe that is not up to them to disobey them. Surah 24:2 instructs Muslims not to let compassion cause them to disobey what Allah has prescribed.

Many Muslims regard capital punishment as an effective deterrent, and protection for society

Muslim attitudes against the death penalty

Although a minority view, some Muslims are against the death penalty

They argue that Islam is a religion of peace, and capital punishment is a violent act. The Qur'an does not make capital punishment compulsory, but offers a chance, in the case of murder, for the victim's family to forgive and take a payment of blood money instead:

> *"If any remission is made to anyone by his aggrieved brother, then prosecution [for the murder] should be made according to usage, and payment should be made to him in a good manner; this is an alleviation from your Lord and a mercy."*
>
> **Surah 2:178**

There is sometimes disagreement between scholars about when and if to apply capital punishment and the application of sacred texts

Some Muslims argue that, in response to surah 4:65, surah 4:137 says that there are people who believe, then disbelieve, then believe again, but who are not executed; it notes that Allah will never forgive them, but does not indicate that their lives have been, or should be, taken.

The idea that the death penalty is a deterrent is disputed

There is not convincing statistical evidence that this is the case. Life imprisonment would also protect society, and uphold justice.

There are mixed non-religious views about capital punishment. These depend on what type of punishment is thought to be the most effective. If a person thinks punishment should act as a deterrent or as retribution, then capital punishment might be supported. If such punishments are regarded as vengeful, and lacking in justice, then capital punishment will not be seen as an appropriate form of punishment.

Non-religious attitudes for the death penalty

- **DETERRENT** - The threat of capital punishment can act as a deterrent in society

- **THREAT REMOVAL** - Taking a criminal's life, when they have committed a serious crime, permanently removes them as a threat to society

- **FAMILY JUSTICE** - Taking a life in retribution can bring a sense of justice to the victim's family

- **VALUES LIFE** - Taking the life of a murderer says how seriously life is valued; if the murderer has taken life, the only fitting punishment is for their life to be taken

Non-religious attitudes against the death penalty

- **LITTLE EVIDENCE** - That the death penalty has any significant deterrent effect; people do not necessarily think about the punishment in the heat of committing a serious crime

- **REVENGE IS DESTRUCTIVE** - It legitimises violence, and does not belong in a civilised society. It does not honour human rights or allow for dignity

- **ONLY SPREADS PAIN** - Capital punishment does not necessarily bring a sense of justice and relief to the victim's family but only spreads pain to the family of the person who committed the crime

- **HYPOCRITICAL** - Society and the law cannot say taking a life is wrong and then take a life itself

The Humanist Society is against capital punishment:

"Capital punishment is generally opposed by humanists because they think premeditated killing is wrong, even when carried out by the state, and because of the possibility of error and an irrevocable failure of justice."

Muslim responses

- **THE QUR'AN ALLOWS FOR CASES** - in which capital punishment should be carried out, and this is the ultimate authority for human beings. Allah's ways are just and perfect, and establish truth and peace

- **RESPECT FOR HUMAN LIFE IS GIVEN IN ISLAM** - in agreement with non-religious views - but when a person has taken a life or committed certain other crimes against Allah, they have lost the right to continue their own life